THE
AVOCADO
COOKBOOK

10 9 8

Ebury Press, an imprint of Ebury Publishing,
20 Vauxhall Bridge Road,
London SW1V 2SA

Ebury Press is part of the Penguin Random House group of companies
whose addresses can be found at global.penguinrandomhouse.com

Penguin
Random House
UK

First published by Ebury Publishing in 2016

www.eburypublishing.co.uk

A CIP catalogue record for this book is available from the British Library

ISBN 9781785033988

Printed and bound in Italy by Printer Trento S.r.l.

Penguin Random House is committed to a sustainable future for our
business, our readers and our planet. This book is made from Forest
Stewardship Council® certified paper.

Design: Louise Evans
Photography: Joff Lee
Food stylist: Mari Williams
Project editor: Lydia Good

THE
AVOCADO
COOKBOOK

EBURY
PRESS

CONTENTS

MAIN MEALS

DESSERTS & DRINKS

INTRODUCTION

Avocados, with their velvety, buttery texture and mild nutty flavour, are one of the so-called 'superfoods'. Contrary to what most people think, this smooth- or rough-skinned delicacy is technically a fruit, not a vegetable. Avocados are available in many shapes, colours and sizes – they can be dark green, purplish brown or black-skinned; round or oval; 'baby' or large. There are many varieties available, of which the most common are the Hass (black wrinkled skin) and the Fuerte (green leathery skin), but the flavour of the fruit does not vary.

ORIGINS AND HISTORY

The avocado is native to Central America and is widely used in Mexican cookery – its name is derived from the ancient Aztec word *ahuacatl* (meaning 'testicle', which it was thought to resemble) and the later Spanish version, *aguacate*. The Spanish conquistadors, who discovered the fruit when they conquered and colonised the region, liked it so much that they shipped avocado tree saplings to other subtropical areas. Avocados are now widely cultivated in Spain, Israel, South Africa, Indonesia and Australia as well as Peru, Mexico, the Caribbean and California, and they are shipped all over the world.

NUTRITIONAL AND HEALTH BENEFITS

Avocados are among the most nutritious foods you can eat. Not only are they rich in protein and fibre but they are also a good source of potassium, magnesium, iron, zinc, folic acid and vitamins A, B3, B5, B6, B12, C, E and K. They are particularly good for promoting healthy skin, aiding digestion and preventing anaemia. Eating them regularly in pregnancy is thought to prevent stretch marks.

Because they are relatively high in fat, many weight-conscious people avoid them, but in fact they contain healthy polyunsaturated and monounsaturated vegetable fat. And they don't contain any cholesterol either. Indeed, some studies have shown that eating avocados regularly may help to lower harmful cholesterol levels and reduce the risk of developing heart disease. The oil can be extracted from the fruits and is available in bottles for cooking or using in salad dressings.

STORING AND RIPENING AVOCADOS

Avocados ripen best off the tree and can be bought 'ready to eat' or while they are still hard, then stored in the refrigerator (if you want to slow down the ripening process) or at room temperature. Keeping them in a brown paper bag with an apple or a banana helps to speed up the ripening process, so they should be ready to eat in two to three days. They are ripe if they yield slightly when you press the skin gently with a finger.

PREPARING AVOCADOS

Avocados discolour quickly and easily when they are cut open and exposed to the air. You can delay this oxidisation process by sprinkling the cut flesh with a little lemon or lime juice. Otherwise, prepare them at the last minute just before serving. Cut them in half lengthways and discard the stone (pit). Either scoop out the flesh with a teaspoon or carefully remove the peel and cut into neat slices or cubes. If you're going to fill the avocados or eat them as they are, brush the cut surface lightly with lemon, lime or even orange juice. If you have an unused leftover half of avocado, sprinkle it with an acidic agent, such as lemon juice, and wrap tightly in cling film (plastic wrap). Keep in the refrigerator for up to 24 hours before using.

FLAVOURINGS

Avocados have a subtle and delicate flavour, reminiscent of hazelnuts. They are neither sweet nor bitter and in Mexico and the Caribbean they are usually flavoured with hot chillies, spices, salt and garlic, and served with tomatoes and corn tortillas. They have become a staple of Tex-Mex food. They also complement chicken, seafood and shellfish, and their creamy, silky texture offsets beans and pulses perfectly. You can eat them plain and raw with a pinch of crushed sea salt, a drizzle of vinaigrette or a few drops of good balsamic vinegar, or you can cook them in a variety of recipes.

USING AND COOKING AVOCADOS

Avocados are extremely versatile and are delicious served hot or cold in so many ways. As well as their most common and well-known use as the staple ingredient in guacamole, the spicy Mexican dip, they can be added to sandwiches, salads, rice, pasta and grains and even made into chilled soups, sauces, smoothies, desserts and ice cream. They can be griddled, mashed and piled onto toast, or filled with a savoury mixture and baked in the oven or finished off under a hot grill (broiler). Or you can enjoy them the Californian way by mashing them and mixing into a vinaigrette salad dressing. You will find recipes for all these dishes and more in this book.

BREAKFASTS & BRUNCHES

MEXICAN BRUNCH BURRITOS

SERVES: 2 | **PREP:** 10 MINUTES | **COOK:** 6–8 MINUTES

2 large multi-seed or multi-grain tortilla wraps
1 tbsp olive oil
4 spring onions (scallions), diced
1 red chilli, deseeded and diced
6 cherry tomatoes, chopped
3 medium eggs
2 tbsp chopped coriander (cilantro)
1 ripe avocado
2 tbsp low-fat sour cream
salt and freshly ground black pepper

This quick and easy breakfast can be piled on top of a tortilla and then rolled up and eaten by hand. It's a great nutritious way to start the day. Choose multi-seed or multi-grain wraps – they have more fibre than regular flour or corn ones.

1 Heat the tortillas in a low oven or on a hot griddle (grill) pan, according to packet instructions.

2 In a non-stick frying pan (skillet), heat the oil and gently cook the spring onions, chilli and tomatoes for 3–4 minutes.

3 Whisk the eggs and seasoning in a bowl with the coriander. Pour into the hot pan and stir over a low heat until they start to scramble and set. Take care not to overcook them.

4 Halve, stone (pit) and peel the avocado and cut the flesh into dice.

5 Divide the scrambled egg mixture between the warm tortillas and top with the avocado and sour cream. Fold over or roll up and eat straight away.

OR YOU CAN TRY THIS...

– For a more slimming version, substitute low-fat natural yoghurt for the sour cream and use smaller wraps or reduced-fat ones.
– Instead of adding diced avocado to the burritos, use guacamole (see recipe on page 24).
– If you like your burritos with a bit of heat, top them with a spoonful of hot salsa.
– If you're feeling really hungry, sprinkle some grated Cheddar or Monterey Jack cheese over the top, or stir it into the scrambled egg mixture.

EGG & BACON BREAKFAST SALAD

SERVES: 2 | **PREP:** 10 MINUTES | **COOK:** 6 MINUTES

2 rashers (slices) smoked
    back bacon
1 tsp white wine vinegar
2 medium eggs
1 ripe avocado
8 baby plum tomatoes,
    halved
4 spring onions (scallions),
    thinly sliced
100g/4oz (4 cups) rocket
    (arugula), baby spinach
    or mixed salad leaves
3 tbsp vinaigrette or
    balsamic dressing
salt and freshly ground black
    pepper
toasted ciabatta or
    sourdough, to serve

This is an unusual and healthy twist on the more familiar egg and bacon fry up. It's not only delicious and refreshing but more slimming than the original, too. Don't be alarmed at the idea of adding vinegar to the poaching water for the eggs; it doesn't affect their flavour but it does help to coagulate the protein in the egg whites.

1 Heat a non-stick frying pan (skillet) and dry-fry the bacon for 2–3 minutes until crisp and golden brown. Remove and drain on kitchen paper (paper towels).

2 Heat some water in a pan to simmering point. Add the vinegar and then gently break in the eggs. Cook very gently for about 3 minutes until the whites are set but the yolks are still runny.

3 While the eggs are cooking, halve, stone (pit) and peel the avocado. Slice the flesh thinly and mix with the tomatoes, spring onions and salad leaves in a bowl, then toss lightly in the dressing of your choice. Divide between 2 serving plates.

4 Carefully remove the poached eggs from the pan with a slotted spoon and place one on top of each salad. Season lightly with salt and pepper and crumble the crispy bacon over the top. Serve at once while the eggs are warm, with toasted bread.

OR YOU CAN TRY THIS...
– Dry-fry thin slices of Parma ham and add to the salad instead of bacon.
– Vegetarians can omit the bacon and add some diced feta cheese or even vegetarian bacon-style rashers, such as Quorn.
– Experiment with different flavours: try adding chopped herbs, diced red onion, grilled red and yellow (bell) pepper strips or some crisp croûtons.

PAPRIKA FRENCH TOAST

SERVES: 2 | **PREP:** 10 MINUTES | **COOK:** 4–6 MINUTES

6 rashers (slices) thin-cut
    streaky bacon or pancetta
2 medium eggs
2–3 tbsp milk
2 thick slices wholemeal
    or multi-grain bread
1 tsp olive oil
15g/½oz/1 tbsp unsalted
    butter
1 ripe avocado
juice of ½ lemon (1 tbsp)
good pinch of smoked
    paprika
salt and freshly ground
    black pepper
maple syrup, to serve

Bacon and avocado makes a great combo and here they are also paired with a savoury version of French toast for a delicious weekend breakfast or brunch. This is a good way to use up the end of a loaf of bread that's past its best.

1 Grill or dry-fry the bacon or pancetta in a non-stick frying pan (skillet) until crispy and golden.

2 Beat the eggs with the milk in a shallow bowl, and season lightly with salt and pepper. Dip in the bread and turn it over in the beaten egg mixture. Leave for 2–3 minutes to soak up all the liquid.

3 Heat the olive oil and butter in a large non-stick frying pan (skillet) over a medium heat. When hot, add the soaked slices of bread to the pan and cook for 2–3 minutes on each side until golden brown. Remove carefully.

4 Meanwhile, halve, stone (pit) and peel the avocado and cut the flesh into dice. Sprinkle the avocado with the lemon juice and seasoning to taste.

5 Place a slice of French toast on each serving plate and dust with the smoked paprika. Pile the avocado and bacon or pancetta on top and serve immediately with the maple syrup alongside.

OR YOU CAN TRY THIS...
– Sliced brioche, baguette (french stick) or even halved bagels can be used instead of sliced bread.
– For a more substantial breakfast, serve the French toast with a sliced banana.
– If you have a sweet tooth, omit the paprika and sprinkle with cinnamon. Serve with fresh berries (blueberries, raspberries and strawberries) or fruit compôte and a dollop of 0% fat Greek yoghurt.

BALSAMIC ROASTED TOMATO & AVOCADO TOASTIES

SERVES: 2 | **PREP:** 5 MINUTES | **COOK:** 1 HOUR

3 tomatoes
1 tsp balsamic vinegar
olive oil, for drizzling
1 ripe avocado
juice of ½ lemon (1 tbsp)
2 thick slices sourdough
    or multi-seed bread
sea salt and freshly ground
    black pepper
few chives, snipped,
    to serve

Sticky, slightly caramelised slow-roasted tomatoes are delicious and extremely versatile, so it's worth trebling the quantity given below and cooking some extra to toss with hot pasta, say, or to use as a garnish for a puréed vegetable soup.

1 Preheat the oven to 170°C, 325°F, gas mark 3.

2 Cut the tomatoes in half and place them, cut side up, on a baking tray. Sprinkle with balsamic vinegar and drizzle with olive oil. Grind a little sea salt and black pepper over the top and bake in the oven for 1 hour.

3 Cut the avocado in half, remove the stone (pit) and scoop out the flesh. Using a fork, mash it roughly with the lemon juice and some salt.

4 Toast the bread and spread with the mashed avocado. Arrange the roasted tomatoes on top and sprinkle with the chives.

OR YOU CAN TRY THIS...
– If you like garlic, add some crushed cloves to the tomatoes before roasting, or even mash a raw clove with the avocado.
– Lime juice works well if you don't have a spare lemon.
– Instead of topping the avocado toasties with tomatoes, try grilled or sweet pepperdew peppers, a spoonful of hot salsa or a drizzle of sweet chilli sauce. Thin-sliced smoked salmon or Parma ham are great, too, as is diced chorizo.
– Spread the toast with some chilli jam or spicy chutney before adding the avocado.
– Drizzle lightly with Tabasco, harissa or chilli oil.

SCRAMBLED EGG & AVOCADO TOASTIES

SERVES: 2 | **PREP:** 5 MINUTES | **COOK:** 4–5 MINUTES

3 medium eggs
1 tbsp milk
1 ripe avocado
juice of ½ lime (1 tbsp)
few sprigs of parsley or
    coriander (cilantro),
    chopped
75g/3oz (½ cup) soft
    creamy goat's cheese
2 thick slices wholegrain
    bread
15g/½oz/1 tbsp butter, plus
    extra for spreading
salt and freshly ground black
    pepper
few dried chilli flakes

This avocado toastie is a great way to kick-start your day. It's so nutritious; the eggs and cheese provide you with protein as well as essential minerals and vitamins.

1 Beat the eggs and milk together with a little seasoning in a bowl.

2 Cut the avocado in half, remove the stone (pit) and scoop out the flesh. Roughly mash the flesh with the lime juice. Stir in the herbs and goat's cheese and season to taste.

3 Toast the bread and lightly butter it. Pile the avocado and cheese mixture on top.

4 Melt the remaining butter in a small non-stick frying pan (skillet) and place over a low–medium heat. When the butter melts, add the beaten eggs and stir with a wooden spoon until they scramble and start to set. Remove from the heat immediately.

5 Spoon the scrambled egg on top of the avocado toasts and dust lightly with the chilli flakes. Eat immediately.

OR YOU CAN TRY THIS...

– Spice this up by adding some finely diced chilli to the mashed avocado.
– For a more slimming version, use extra-light soft cheese – some brands have only a quarter of the calories and fat grams of full-fat cream cheese.
– Make the scrambled eggs more interesting by adding finely chopped herbs, diced tomato and spring onions (scallions).
– Try poaching or frying a couple of eggs until the whites are set but the yolks are still runny. Place an egg on top of each avocado toastie. You can also add a rasher (slice) of grilled (broiled) or dry-fried bacon.
– Serve on toasted muffins, bagels or crumpets instead of bread.
– Dust with some hot cayenne pepper or smoked paprika. And, if you haven't got a lime, you can use lemon juice instead.

AVOCADO BAKED EGGS

SERVES: 2 | **PREP:** 5 MINUTES | **COOK:** 15–20 MINUTES

1 large ripe avocado
2 small eggs
pinch of paprika or cayenne
    pepper
2 rashers (slices) thin-cut
    bacon
2 tsp chopped parsley
    or chives
salt and freshly ground
    black pepper
toasted bread, to serve

If you've never tried eating baked avocado, now's your chance. This makes a fabulous cooked breakfast, brunch or supper dish… and it's so simple to make.

1 Preheat the oven to 180°C, 350°F, gas mark 4.

2 Cut the avocado in half and remove the stone (pit). Carefully scoop out a little of the flesh to make room for the eggs.

3 Place the avocados in a small ovenproof dish or into 2 individual ramekins. It's important that they fit quite tightly to prevent them toppling over and the liquid egg spilling out.

4 Carefully break an egg into each avocado half. Make sure you add the whole yolks and most, if not all, of the white – as much as you can get into the space without it overflowing. Sprinkle with a little paprika or cayenne, plus salt and pepper.

5 Bake in the oven for 15–20 minutes until the whites are set.

6 Meanwhile, heat the grill (broiler) or a frying pan (skillet) and grill (broil) or dry-fry the bacon until crisp and golden. Sprinkle the baked avocado eggs with the chopped herbs, top with the bacon and serve with toast.

OR YOU CAN TRY THIS…

– If you like it hot, sprinkle the cooked eggs with dried chilli flakes or a dash of Tabasco or chilli sauce.
– Instead of bacon, scatter with diced cooked chorizo or spicy sausage.
– For a vegetarian alternative, leave out the bacon and sprinkle with diced tomato. Or cover with grated cheese towards the end of the cooking time and pop back into the oven until it melts.

SNACKS & LIGHT MEALS

GUACAMOLE

SERVES: 4 | **PREP:** 10 MINUTES

½ red onion, diced
1 fresh green chilli, diced
½ tsp sea salt crystals
1 garlic clove, crushed
2 ripe avocados
juice of 1 lime
1 small bunch coriander
  (cilantro), chopped
1 ripe tomato, deseeded
  and diced
freshly ground black pepper

This classic Mexican dip is so simple to make and takes no time at all. It tastes so much better than the ready-made sort. Its name is derived from two Aztec words: *guac* (avocado) and *mole* (sauce).

1 Crush the red onion, chilli and salt with a pestle and mortar.

2 Cut the avocados in half and remove the stones (pits). Scoop out the flesh and mash roughly with a fork – it shouldn't be too smooth. Stir in the lime juice.

3 Add the coriander, crushed red onion mixture and the tomato to the mashed avocado and mix everything together. Add a grinding of black pepper and spoon into a serving bowl.

200g salted corn tortilla
  chips
4 tomatoes, deseeded
  and chopped
400g/14oz can kidney
  beans, rinsed and drained
1 bunch spring onions
  (scallions), chopped
2 fresh green chillies,
  deseeded and diced
100g/4oz (1 cup) grated
  Cheddar cheese
150g/5oz (1 cup) hot salsa
1 quantity guacamole
  (see above)

CHEESY NACHOS WITH GUACAMOLE

SERVES: 4 | **PREP:** 5 MINUTES | **COOK:** 10 MINUTES

This is a great party dish. You can serve it with drinks before dinner or as part of a hot buffet. It's more Tex-Mex than authentic Mexican, but no matter – it tastes fabulous!

1 Preheat the oven to 200°C, 400°F, gas mark 6.

2 Put the tortilla chips in an ovenproof dish and scatter with the tomatoes, beans, spring onions and chillies. Sprinkle with the grated cheese.

3 Bake in the oven for about 10 minutes until the cheese melts and is bubbling.

4 Spoon the salsa and guacamole over the top and serve immediately.

CAJUN SWEET POTATO WEDGES WITH GUACAMOLE

SERVES: 4 | **PREP:** 10 MINUTES | **COOK:** 20–30 MINUTES

500g/1lb 2oz sweet potatoes
spray olive oil
1 tbsp ground black
    peppercorns
1 tbsp paprika
1 tsp cayenne pepper
good pinch of chilli powder
1 tbsp dried mixed herbs
1 tbsp soft brown sugar
good pinch of fine sea salt,
    plus extra for sprinkling
freshly ground black pepper
1 quantity guacamole
    (see page 24)

You can enjoy these spicy sweet potatoes as a snack, a party dish or even as an accompaniment to grilled chicken, steak or sausages.

1 Preheat the oven to 200°C, 400°F, gas mark 6.

2 Scrub the sweet potatoes and cut them into wedges. Spray lightly with olive oil.

3 Mix together the spices, herbs, sugar and salt. Add the sweet potato wedges and coat them with the spicy mixture. Arrange them on a non-stick baking sheet.

4 Cook in the oven for 20–30 minutes until the sweet potatoes are tender inside and crisp and golden brown on the outside.

5 Serve hot, sprinkled with sea salt and black pepper, with the guacamole dip alongside.

OR YOU CAN TRY THIS...

– For a smoky flavour, cook the sweet potatoes on a hot barbecue for 20–25 minutes.
– Coat the sweet potatoes with a mixture of 2 tbsp curry paste, juice of ½ lemon, 1 tsp olive oil and 2 tbsp low-fat natural yoghurt. Bake in the oven as above.

SPROUTED BEAN & AVOCADO SALAD

SERVES: 4 | **PREP:** 10 MINUTES | **COOK:** 5–6 MINUTES

175g/6oz streaky bacon
    rashers (slices), rind
    removed
175g/6oz mixed salad
    leaves, e.g. frisée (curly
    endive), oak leaf, cos,
    batavia
50g/2oz salad sprouts
25g/1oz alfalfa sprouts
25g/1oz mustard and cress
1 ripe avocado

Dressing:
2 tsp raspberry vinegar
1 tsp wholegrain mustard
1 tsp grated fresh root
    ginger
¼ tsp clear honey
4 tbsp walnut oil
2 tbsp sunflower oil
salt and freshly ground
    black pepper

Sprouted beans and seeds are available from many supermarkets as well as health-food stores. They are full of goodness and add a delightful bite to this vibrant salad.

1 Make the dressing: in a small bowl, whisk together the vinegar, mustard, ginger and honey. Gradually whisk in the oils, then season with salt and pepper to taste.

2 Preheat the grill (broiler). Place the bacon on a foil-lined grill pan and grill (broil) for 2–3 minutes each side until crisp and golden. When cool, break into bite-sized pieces.

3 Place the salad leaves, sprouts and mustard and cress in a large bowl. Add a little of the dressing and toss gently to coat the leaves.

4 Halve, stone (pit) and peel the avocado, then cut the flesh into thin slices. Arrange the salad leaves and sprouts on individual serving plates and top with the avocado and crispy bacon pieces. Drizzle over the remaining dressing and serve.

OR YOU CAN TRY THIS...

– Dry-fried thin slices of Parma ham make a change from bacon and have less calories and grams of fat.
– You can eat this salad all the year round – in the winter, sprinkle it with pomegranate seeds for a festive touch.
– Vegetarians can omit the bacon and use diced feta or goat's cheese instead.

TIP: To sprout your own seeds, wash a selection of dried beans, e.g. soya (soy), aduki, chickpeas and green lentils. Place them on some damp kitchen paper (paper towels) and leave in a warm, dark place for 3 days, spraying them with water occasionally. Transfer to a spot in direct sunlight and keep the paper moist. Once sprouted, wash and store in a plastic bag in the refrigerator.

SPICY GRILLED AUBERGINE (EGGPLANT) & AVOCADO SALAD

SERVES: 4 | **PREP:** 25 MINUTES, PLUS STANDING | **COOK:** 8–10 MINUTES

4 baby aubergines
  (eggplants), or 2 small
  ones, trimmed
2 tsp sea salt
2 tbsp sweet soy sauce
2 tsp Thai fish sauce
1 tsp sweet chilli sauce
1 tsp lemon juice
½ tsp ground cumin
½ tsp clear honey
150g/5oz thin green beans,
  trimmed
1 ripe avocado
few crisp lettuce leaves, torn
  into bite-sized pieces
juice of ½ lime
sesame seeds, for sprinkling

Dressing:
1 tbsp groundnut (peanut)
  or sunflower (corn) oil
1 tsp sesame oil
1 tbsp lime juice
pinch of sugar

If you've never thought of eating aubergine (eggplant) in a salad before, try this. Grilling (broiling) brings out its wonderful smoky flavour, which complements the fresh zingy quality of the dressing.

1 Cut the baby aubergines in half lengthways; if using small ones, cut into 4 thick slices. Place in a colander set over a plate and sprinkle with the salt. Set aside for 30 minutes to draw out the bitter juices.

2 Meanwhile, mix together the soy, fish and chilli sauces, lemon juice, cumin and honey.

3 Cut the beans into 5cm (2in) lengths. Bring a large pan of lightly salted water to a rolling boil, plunge in the green beans, then return to the boil and cook for 3 minutes until just tender. Immediately drain and refresh the beans under cold running water.

4 Preheat the grill (broiler). Rinse the aubergines thoroughly to remove the salt and pat dry with kitchen paper (paper towels). Place on a rack over the grill pan and brush with the soy sauce mixture. Grill as close to the heat as possible for 2–3 minutes. Turn the slices over, brush with the remaining soy mixture and cook until charred and tender.

5 Whisk the ingredients for the dressing until well blended. Toss the green beans with half of the dressing.

6 Halve, stone (pit) and peel the avocado and cut the flesh into thin slices. Gently toss with the lettuce in the lime juice and divide between 4 serving plates. Top with the aubergine and beans, then drizzle with the remaining dressing. Scatter the sesame seeds over the top and serve.

OR YOU CAN TRY THIS...

– Use the sweet soy glaze for brushing over fish steaks, especially salmon and fresh tuna. It keeps them moist and succulent during cooking.
– Instead of aubergine, you could use grilled (broiled) red (bell) peppers.

PRAWN (SHRIMP), NOODLE & AVOCADO SALAD

SERVES: 2 | **PREP:** 15 MINUTES | **COOK:** 2 MINUTES

75g/3oz thin rice noodles
150g/5oz mangetout
  (snow peas), trimmed
1 red (bell) pepper, deseeded
  and thinly sliced
1 yellow (bell) pepper,
  deseeded and thinly sliced
1 carrot, cut into thin
  matchsticks
2 spring onions (scallions),
  sliced
225g/8oz (generous 1 ½ cups)
  peeled cooked large
  prawns (jumbo shrimp)
1 small bunch of coriander
  (cilantro), chopped
1 ripe avocado
1 tbsp toasted sesame seeds

Dressing:
2 tbsp Thai fish sauce
1 tbsp light soy sauce
1 tbsp sesame oil
juice of 1 lime
1 tbsp sweet chilli sauce
1 Thai red chilli, diced
2 garlic cloves, crushed
1 tbsp palm sugar or light
  brown sugar

This crisp, fresh-tasting salad keeps well in the refrigerator for a few hours. Make it in advance and transfer individual servings to airtight sealed containers to take to work or college for a packed lunch.

1 Put the noodles in a heatproof shallow bowl and pour boiling water over them. Cover with cling film (plastic wrap) and set aside for about 5 minutes until they are just tender but not too soft. Drain, leave to cool and pat dry with kitchen paper (paper towels).

2 Meanwhile, add the mangetout to a pan of boiling water and cook for 2 minutes until just tender. Drain and refresh immediately in a bowl of iced water. Drain and pat dry, then cut each one into 2–3 pieces.

3 Mix the mangetout with the peppers, carrot, spring onions, prawns, coriander and drained noodles.

4 Cut the avocado in half, remove the stone (pit) and peel. Dice the flesh and add to the noodle mixture.

5 Mix all the dressing ingredients together in a bowl or shake in a screwtop jar.

6 Gently toss the salad in the dressing and divide between 2 serving plates. Sprinkle with sesame seeds and serve.

OR YOU CAN TRY THIS...
– Use sugar snap peas instead of mangetout. You can also add halved cherry tomatoes, cucumber matchsticks or blanched thin green beans.
– Use cellophane noodles (glass noodles) instead to give this salad a Vietnamese feel.

CRAB, MANGO & WILD RICE SALAD

SERVES: 2 | **PREP:** 25 MINUTES | **COOK:** 45 MINUTES

50g/2oz (¼ cup) wild rice
50g/2oz (¼ cup) long grain
  white rice
1 ripe avocado
4 spring onions (scallions),
  finely chopped
1 small ripe mango, peeled,
  stoned (pitted) and diced
1 small carrot, grated
225g/8oz (½ cup) white
  and brown crab meat,
  separated
2 tbsp mayonnaise
juice of ½ lime
pinch of cayenne pepper
4 slices baguette
  (French stick)
2 tsp pine nuts, to serve
few sprigs of coriander
  (cilantro), chopped,
  to serve

Dressing:
3 tbsp olive oil
1 tbsp lemon juice
juice of ½ lime (1 tbsp)
1 tsp grated fresh root
  ginger
2 tbsp chopped coriander
  (cilantro)
salt and freshly ground
  black pepper

This crab salad is so delicious that you can serve it as a light lunch or a starter. For maximum flavour, buy a freshly cooked crab rather than using frozen or canned crab meat. If you don't feel confident about preparing it yourself, ask your fishmonger to do it for you.

1 Cook both types of rice separately according to the instructions on the packets. The wild rice will take 35–40 minutes; the long grain rice 12–15 minutes. Drain well.

2 Meanwhile, whisk all the dressing ingredients together in a bowl and season with salt and pepper to taste.

3 Mix the wild rice and long grain rice together in a large bowl. Add half of the dressing, toss gently, then cover and set aside to cool.

4 Halve, stone (pit) and peel the avocado and cut the flesh into dice. Mix the avocado, spring onions, mango and carrot with the cooled rice. Add the white crab meat, then stir in the remaining dressing.

5 Mix the brown crab meat with the mayonnaise, lime juice and cayenne pepper. Toast the bread lightly on both sides and spread with the crab mayonnaise.

6 Divide the crab and rice salad between 2 serving plates and sprinkle over the pine nuts and coriander. Serve with the crab toasts.

OR YOU CAN TRY THIS...

– If you're watching your weight and counting the calories, you can use extra-light mayonnaise.
– Papaya or even pineapple can be substituted for the mango.

PRAWN (SHRIMP) & AVOCADO FRESH SPRING ROLLS

SERVES: 2 | **PREP:** 15 MINUTES | **COOK:** 4 MINUTES

1 tsp coconut oil
1 red (bell) pepper, deseeded and diced
100g/4oz (2 cups) carrots, cut into matchsticks
75g/3oz (¾ cup) spring greens, shredded
100g/4oz (1 cup) beansprouts
150g/5oz (scant 1 cup) cooked peeled prawns (shrimp)
2 tbsp light soy sauce
1 small ripe avocado
3 tbsp chopped coriander (cilantro)
6 rice paper wrappers
sweet chilli sauce, for dipping

These spring rolls are fresh and summery, not like the traditional fried hot ones. You can buy rice paper spring roll wrappers in many supermarkets as well as Asian stores and online.

1 Heat the coconut oil in a non-stick frying pan (skillet) or wok. Stir-fry the red pepper and carrot for 2 minutes. Add the spring greens, beansprouts and prawns and cook for 2 minutes.

2 Stir in the soy sauce and remove from the heat. Halve, stone (pit) and peel the avocado and cut the flesh into dice. Add the avocado and coriander to the stir-fried veg.

3 Dip the rice paper wrappers, one at a time, into a bowl of cold water for about 20 seconds until pliable. Lay one out flat and add a spoonful of the filling. Fold the sides of the wrapper over the filling and roll up like a parcel. Repeat with the rest of the wrappers and filling.

4 Serve the spring rolls immediately with a bowl of chilli sauce for dipping.

OR YOU CAN TRY THIS...

– You can use diced or shredded cooked chicken or pork instead of prawns.
– Leave the prawns out and add extra stir-fried vegetables, such as spring onions (scallions), mushrooms and courgettes (zucchini) plus some chopped salted roasted peanuts.
– Make a dipping sauce with 1 tbsp Thai fish sauce, the juice of a small lime, 1 crushed garlic clove, 1 diced red chilli and a good pinch of sugar.
– Use fresh shredded lettuce instead of stir-fried greens plus some cucumber matchsticks.

SMOKED SALMON & AVOCADO BRUSCHETTA

SERVES: 2 | **PREP:** 15 MINUTES | **COOK:** 2–3 MINUTES

1 ripe avocado
2 tbsp low-fat natural
   yoghurt
squeeze of lime juice
4 slices ciabatta or focaccia
olive oil, for sprinkling
50g/2oz thinly sliced
   smoked salmon
sea salt and freshly ground
   black pepper

Salsa dressing:
1 small tomato, deseeded
   and diced
1 tsp balsamic vinegar
juice of ½ lime
1 mild red chilli, deseeded
   and finely chopped
few fresh chives, snipped

Quick and easy to make, bruschetta are very versatile snacks – and great party food, too, if you use smaller rounds of bread.

1 Cut the avocado in half, discard the stone (pit) and scoop out the flesh. Mash with the yoghurt and lime juice and season to taste with salt and black pepper.

2 Mix all the salsa dressing ingredients together in a bowl or shake in a screwtop jar until well blended.

3 Heat the grill (broiler). Lightly toast the bread on one side only. Lightly spray the untoasted side with oil and grill (broil) until crisp and golden.

4 Spread the mashed avocado over the grilled side of the bread and top with the smoked salmon. Sprinkle with the salsa dressing and serve.

OR YOU CAN TRY THIS...

– Use a potato peeler to shave some long wafer-thin slices off a peeled chunk of cucumber and add to the bruschetta.
– Roast or grill (broil) some sliced aubergine (eggplant), courgette (zucchini) and/or red or yellow (bell) peppers for an alternative vegetarian topping.
– If you're in a hurry, use bottled grilled peppers. Run a cut clove of garlic over the grilled bread before adding the avocado and topping.
– Sprinkle with pine nuts, toasted sesame seeds, chopped dill or mint.
– Use spicy guacamole (see page 24) instead of plain mashed avocado and top with refried beans and chopped coriander (cilantro).

CREAMY PESTO MUSHROOM TOASTS

SERVES: 2 | **PREP:** 10 MINUTES | **COOK:** 5 MINUTES

1 tbsp olive oil, plus extra
for drizzling
200g/7oz (2 cups) chestnut
mushrooms, thinly sliced
2 tbsp green pesto
2 tbsp cream cheese
2 thick slices sourdough
or wholegrain bread
1 garlic clove, halved
1 ripe avocado
salt and freshly ground
black pepper
fresh basil leaves, to serve

Cook this at the weekend for a late breakfast or lazy brunch – it's a
more sophisticated version of the usual grilled mushrooms on toast.

1 Heat the oil in a large frying pan (skillet) over a medium–high heat.
Once it's hot, add the mushrooms and cook for 4–5 minutes, stirring
occasionally, until tender and starting to brown.

2 Reduce the heat under the mushrooms to a simmer and stir in the
pesto and cream cheese. Season to taste with salt and black pepper.

3 Meanwhile, toast the bread and rub with the garlic clove on one side.
Drizzle with a little olive oil.

4 Halve, stone (pit) and peel the avocado. Slice thinly and arrange on
top of the toast.

5 Pile the mushrooms on top, scatter with basil leaves and serve.

OR YOU CAN TRY THIS...

– Instead of cream cheese, stir in some creamy mascarpone or half-fat
crème fraîche.
– If you're health- and calorie-conscious, opt for extra-light soft cheese
as it's much lower in fat. You can buy reduced-calorie pesto, too.
– If you happen to have some fresh wild mushrooms – morels,
chanterelles or ceps – they will elevate this simple dish to a whole
new level of flavour.

SWEETCORN FRITTERS WITH AVOCADO SALSA

SERVES: 2 | **PREP:** 15 MINUTES | **COOK:** 10 MINUTES

100g/4oz (½ cup) canned
    sweetcorn kernels,
    drained
75g/3oz (½ cup) self-raising
    (self-rising) flour
1 medium egg, separated
1–2 tbsp milk
1 bird's eye red chilli,
    deseeded and diced
¼ red onion, finely chopped
few sprigs of coriander
    (cilantro), finely chopped
2 tbsp groundnut (peanut)
    oil
salt and freshly ground
    black pepper
sweet chilli sauce, to serve
lime wedges, to serve

Avocado salsa:
1 ripe avocado
2 tomatoes, diced
½ red onion, diced
1 hot chilli, diced
1 garlic clove, crushed
few sprigs of coriander
    (cilantro), chopped
juice of 1 lime

These colourful fritters are surprisingly easy to make and don't take long. They are very healthy and packed with vitamins, minerals and fibre.

1 Make the avocado salsa. Halve, stone (pit) and peel the avocado and cut it into dice, then mix with all the other salsa ingredients in a bowl and set aside while you make the fritters.

2 Put the sweetcorn in a small pan and cover with a little water. Bring to the boil and cook for 2 minutes. Drain well.

3 Sift the flour into a bowl, add some salt and pepper and make a well in the centre. In a separate bowl, whisk the egg yolk and milk and then beat into the flour until you have a stiff batter.

4 Whisk the egg white in a clean, dry bowl until stiff. Using a metal spoon, fold it gently into the batter in a figure-of-eight movement. Gently stir in the sweetcorn, chilli, red onion and coriander, distributing them evenly throughout the batter.

5 Heat the oil in a non-stick frying pan (skillet) over a high heat. When the pan is hot, add small spoonfuls of the mixture, flattening them a little with a spatula, and cook in batches for about 2 minutes until golden brown underneath. Flip them over and cook the other side.

6 Serve the hot fritters, drizzled with sweet chilli sauce, with the avocado salsa and lime wedges.

OR YOU CAN TRY THIS...
– Use whole corn cobs and simmer for 6–7 minutes before stripping off the kernels and mixing with the other ingredients.
– Substitute finely sliced spring onions (scallions) for the red onion.
– If you don't have any groundnut oil use sunflower (corn) oil instead.
– You can also mix some diced avocado into a tub of ready-made salsa.

CHILLI, CHICKEN & AVOCADO WRAPS

SERVES: 2 | **PREP:** 10 MINUTES | **COOK:** 3 MINUTES

1 tsp sunflower (corn) or groundnut (peanut) oil
100g/4oz (scant 1 cup) roast chicken, skinned and shredded
½ red chilli, deseeded and diced
1cm (½in) piece fresh root ginger, chopped
1 garlic clove, crushed
1 ripe avocado
50g/2oz (½ cup) beansprouts
1 carrot, grated
50g/2oz (2 cups) baby spinach leaves
2 large tortilla wraps
salt and freshly ground black pepper

Dressing:
juice of ½ lime
1 tsp dark soy sauce
2 tsp sesame oil

These delicious wraps can be packed into a lunchbox and taken to work. They're a great way of using up leftovers from the Sunday roast, or you can buy a ready-cooked chicken breast in the supermarket.

1 Heat the oil in a non-stick frying pan (skillet) or wok and add the chicken, chilli, ginger and garlic. Cook briskly over a medium–high heat for 2–3 minutes until the chicken starts to turn golden and the garlic is cooked but not brown.

2 Make the dressing: whisk together the lime juice, soy sauce and sesame oil with seasoning to taste.

3 Halve, stone (pit) and peel the avocado and cut the flesh into dice. Divide the beansprouts, carrot, spinach and avocado between the 2 wraps, then top with the stir-fried chicken. Drizzle over the dressing, roll up and tuck in!

OR YOU CAN TRY THIS...
– Vegetarians can leave out the chicken and add some grated Cheddar cheese, diced feta or mozzarella instead.
– Stir-fried prawns (shrimp) work well too, here.
– Instead of adding diced avocado, top the salad and chicken mixture with a spoonful of guacamole (see page 24).

AVOCADO & CHEESE QUESADILLAS

SERVES: 2 | **PREP:** 10 MINUTES | **COOK:** 6–8 MINUTES

100g/4oz (1 cup) grated
    Cheddar cheese
4 spring onions (scallions),
    thinly sliced
1 red chilli, diced
handful of coriander
    (cilantro), chopped
1 small ripe avocado
juice of ½ lime (1 tbsp)
2 large tortilla wraps
olive oil, for frying
salt and freshly ground
    black pepper
salsa and sour cream,
    to serve

Quesadillas sound very exotic but really they're the Mexican version of toasted sandwiches – and they're just as easy to make. Crisp and golden on the outside and oozing with melted cheese, they are the ultimate snack and comfort food.

1 In a bowl, mix together the cheese, spring onions, chilli and coriander. Season lightly with salt and pepper.

2 Halve, stone (pit) and peel the avocado and cut the flesh into dice. Squeeze the lime juice over the avocado and gently stir into the cheesy mixture.

3 Spread the mixture over 1 tortilla but not right up to the edge. Place the other tortilla on top and press the halves firmly together.

4 Heat a little oil – just a drizzle – in a non-stick frying pan (skillet) over a medium heat. When the pan is hot, carefully add the tortilla and cook for 3–4 minutes until it's golden and crisp underneath.

5 Use a slice (spatula) to flip it over and cook the other side. The filling should be heated through and the cheese melting.

6 Slide the quesadilla out of the pan and cut into 6 wedges. Serve immediately with salsa and some sour cream.

OR YOU CAN TRY THIS...
– Add some shredded cooked chicken, diced ham, chorizo or cooked cubed pancetta to the filling.
– Bottled jalapeño chillies can be substituted for fresh ones.
– Try a filling of refried beans, diced chilli and grated cheese. Serve with guacamole (see page 24).
– Grated mozzarella melts well and makes a change from Cheddar. If you're calorie-conscious, use a reduced-fat version of these cheeses.

CHICKEN & AVOCADO CLUB SANDWICH

SERVES: 2 | **PREP:** 10 MINUTES | **COOK:** 5 MINUTES

4 rashers (slices) lean smoked back bacon
6 slices sourdough or thick-cut white bread
2 tbsp mayonnaise
1 tsp Dijon mustard
100g/4oz grilled chicken breast, skinned and sliced
few crisp lettuce leaves, shredded
1 tomato, sliced
1 ripe avocado
salt and freshly ground black pepper
potato crisps (chips) and sliced gherkins (dill pickles), to serve

This loaded triple-decker sandwich is more of a meal than a snack. The secret of making a good club sandwich is to use the best-quality bread and the freshest ingredients for the filling.

1 Grill (broil) or dry-fry the bacon in a non-stick frying pan (skillet) until crisp and golden.

2 Lightly toast the bread.

3 Mix the mayonnaise with the mustard and spread thinly over each slice of toast. Top 2 slices with the chicken, lettuce and tomato. Season lightly with salt and pepper.

4 Cover each stack with a slice of toast, mayonnaise side up. Halve, stone (pit) and peel the avocado, slice it thinly and lay the slices on top with the bacon. Grind over a little black pepper.

5 Top with the remaining toast, mayonnaise side down, and press down firmly. Secure with cocktail sticks (toothpicks) and cut each sandwich stack diagonally both ways into quarters. Serve immediately with crisps and gherkins.

OR YOU CAN TRY THIS...

– Use wholewheat, granary or multi-grain bread – it's not traditional but it's very healthy and has more fibre than white bread.
– Add thinly sliced Cheddar, Emmenthal or Jarlsberg cheese.
– For a vegetarian club sandwich, layer grilled (broiled) Portobello mushrooms or roasted vegetables – peppers, aubergine (eggplant), courgettes (zucchini) – with the avocado and spread the toast with some hummous.
– Substitute grilled (broiled) halloumi cheese or sliced tofu for the chicken.

STARTERS

AVOCADO & PRAWN (SHRIMP) SUSHI

SERVES: 4–6 | **PREP:** 20 MINUTES | **COOK:** 10–15 MINUTES

300g/10oz (1¼ cups)
  sushi rice
2 tbsp rice vinegar
1 tsp sugar
100g/4oz (¾ cup) peeled
  cooked prawns (shrimp),
  roughly chopped
1–2 tsp wasabi
4 sheets nori seaweed
1 ripe avocado
small bunch of chives
sweet soy sauce, to serve

If you're a sushi fan, why not try making some yourself at home? You can prepare it in advance, it's surprisingly simple and it looks really impressive.

1 Cook the rice according to the directions on the packet – it will take 10–15 minutes until it's tender and all the water has been absorbed. Stir in the vinegar and sugar, then cover the pan and set aside until the rice is at room temperature.

2 Mix the chopped prawns with the wasabi in a bowl – add 1 teaspoon wasabi and taste before adding the second; it is very hot.

3 Place the nori sheets, shiny side down, on a sushi mat or work surface covered with cling film (plastic wrap). Divide the cooled rice between the sheets, spreading it out evenly but not right up to the edges. Leave a 1cm (½in) border along the long edges.

4 Halve, stone (pit) and peel the avocado and slice it thinly. Arrange the wasabi prawns on top of the rice and cover with the long chives and then the sliced avocado.

5 Using the cling film (plastic wrap) and sushi mat (if using) to help you, lift the long bottom edge over the filling and roll up towards the top, pressing down firmly as you do so. When you get to the top, you may need to brush the nori lightly with some water to seal it. Repeat with the other sheets to make 4 rolls.

6 Leave to rest, wrapped in cling film (plastic wrap), for at least 5 minutes or chill until ready to serve.

7 To serve, slice each roll into 8 rounds. Serve with sweet soy sauce for sprinkling or dipping.

OR YOU CAN TRY THIS...

– Use thinly sliced smoked salmon instead of prawns.
– Instead of slicing the avocado, try mashing it with the wasabi and some lemon juice.
– Add some very thinly sliced cucumber, cut lengthways.

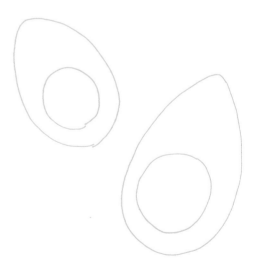

TORTILLA BASKETS

SERVES: 4 | **PREP:** 15 MINUTES | **COOK:** 8–10 MINUTES

olive oil, for brushing
4 soft flour tortillas
1 ripe avocado
8 ripe cherry tomatoes,
    halved
1 yellow (bell) pepper,
    deseeded and chopped
½ red onion, diced
1 hot chilli, diced
few baby salad leaves,
    torn into pieces
150g/5oz (1 cup) cooked
    chicken breast, skinned
    and diced, or ripped
salt and freshly ground
    black pepper
salsa, to serve
chopped coriander
    (cilantro), to serve

Dressing:
3 tbsp olive oil
1 tbsp white wine or
    cider vinegar
juice and grated zest
    of 1 lime
pinch of sugar

These crisp tortilla baskets make an unusual and pretty first course. Prepare the 'baskets' in advance and add the salad just before serving.

1 Preheat the oven to 200°C, 400°F, gas mark 6.

2 Lightly brush 4 Yorkshire-pudding moulds (extra-large muffin pans), or 4 small ramekins, with oil. Press the tortillas down into the moulds to make a basket shape. Bake in the oven for 8–10 minutes, until crisp and golden. Check during cooking to make sure that they do not over-brown. Remove and set aside to cool.

3 Mix the dressing ingredients together in a small bowl.

4 Halve, stone (pit) and peel the avocado and cut the flesh into dice. In a separate bowl, mix together the avocado, tomatoes, yellow pepper, red onion, chilli, salad leaves and chicken. Toss gently in the dressing and season to taste.

5 Divide the chicken and avocado salad mixture between the tortilla baskets and top with a spoonful of salsa and some chopped coriander.

OR YOU CAN TRY THIS...

– Instead of mixing diced avocado into the salad filling, top the salad with a large spoonful of guacamole (see page 24).
– Mash the avocado and a crushed garlic clove into the vinaigrette dressing and toss the salad leaves in it.
– Substitute prawns (shrimp) for the chicken.
– For a vegetarian version, leave out the chicken and add some diced cheese, chickpeas, kidney beans or roasted vegetables.

GRIDDLED AVOCADO WITH SALMON

SERVES: 4 | **PREP:** 10 MINUTES | **COOK:** 3–4 MINUTES

150g/5oz smoked salmon,
  finely chopped
150g/5oz (scant 1 cup)
  soft cheese
2 tbsp crème fraîche
1 tsp creamed horseradish
grated zest of 1 lemon,
  juice of ½
small bunch of dill, chopped
2 ripe avocados
freshly ground black pepper
salad leaves and vinaigrette,
  to serve

The smoked salmon topping can be prepared in advance and kept in a sealed container in the refrigerator until you are ready to cook the avocados, just before serving. Choose avocados that are just ripe but still a little firm – not too soft.

1 In a bowl, mix together the smoked salmon, soft cheese, crème fraîche and horseradish. Add the lemon zest and juice and then stir in most of the dill, keeping a few leaves for the garnish. Season to taste with black pepper.

2 Cut the avocados in half and remove the stones.

3 Place a lightly oiled, ridged non-stick griddle (grill) pan over a high heat and when it's hot, add the avocado halves, cut-side down, pressing lightly on them so they make contact with the ridges of the pan. Cook for 3–4 minutes until they start to soften and charred stripes appear.

4 Remove the avocados and top each one with a spoonful of the smoked salmon mixture. Sprinkle with the remaining dill and a grinding of black pepper. Serve immediately with a few salad leaves, drizzled with vinaigrette.

OR YOU CAN TRY THIS...

– Use sour cream instead of soft cheese, or extra-light soft cheese if you want to reduce the calories.
– Hot smoked salmon is less salty and oily than smoked. Flake it and add to the horseradish-soft cheese mixture with some grated lime zest and juice.
– Use small cooked prawns (shrimp) instead of salmon, and substitute snipped chives for the dill.
– As an alternative garnish, use some salmon lumpfish caviar roe or sprinkle with cayenne pepper.
– In the summer, try cooking the avocados on the oiled bars of a hot barbecue for a really smoky flavour.

CRISP CHEESY BAKED AVOCADOS

SERVES: 4 | **PREP:** 15 MINUTES | **COOK:** 15 MINUTES

2 large ripe avocados
75g/3oz sun-blush
 tomatoes, drained and
 chopped
4 baby plum tomatoes,
 diced
50g/2oz (½ cup) pine nuts
few sprigs of parsley, finely
 chopped
1–2 tbsp green pesto
4 tbsp fresh breadcrumbs
2 tbsp grated Parmesan
 cheese
olive oil, for drizzling
salt and freshly ground
 black pepper
rocket (arugula) or frisée
 (curly endive), to serve
1 tsp vinaigrette dressing,
 to serve

Baked avocados make a really quick and easy starter or snack, and can be bumped up to make a light meal if you serve them with a crisp salad and allow two halves per person.

1 Preheat the oven to 200°C, 400°F, gas mark 6.

2 Cut the avocados in half lengthways and discard the stones (pits). Hollow them out a little with a teaspoon and put the scooped-out flesh in a bowl with the sun-blush tomatoes, baby plum tomatoes, pine nuts, parsley and pesto. Season lightly with salt and pepper and mix together.

3 Fill the avocado halves with this mixture and stand them in an ovenproof dish – they should fit snugly so they can't topple over during cooking.

4 Sprinkle the tops with the breadcrumbs and Parmesan. Drizzle a little olive oil over the top and bake in the oven for about 10–15 minutes until crisp and golden brown.

5 Serve hot, garnished with rocket or frisée and sprinkled with vinaigrette.

OR YOU CAN TRY THIS...
– Omit the Parmesan and add some diced feta, mozzarella or goat's cheese to the filling ingredients.
– Fill the avocado halves with salsa, top with the breadcrumbs and Parmesan and bake as above.
– Leave out the pesto and parsley, and add some diced chilli and chopped coriander (cilantro). Sprinkle with breadcrumbs and grated Cheddar cheese and cook as above.

THAI GRILLED AVOCADO WITH CRAB & MANGO

SERVES: 2 | **PREP:** 15 MINUTES | **COOK:** 3–4 MINUTES

350g/12oz (1 cup) mixed crab meat (white and brown)
2 spring onions (scallions), diced
1 green chilli, diced
1 red (bell) pepper, deseeded and diced
1 small mango, peeled, stoned (pitted) and diced
few sprigs of coriander (cilantro), chopped, plus extra for sprinkling
2 ripe avocados

Dressing:
1 tbsp Thai fish sauce
juice of 2 limes
1 tbsp palm sugar

This pretty dish makes a great spring or summer starter when fresh crab is in season. If it's not available, you can use frozen or even canned meat instead, with only minimal loss of texture and flavour.

1 In a bowl, mix together the crab meat, spring onions, chilli, red pepper, mango and coriander.

2 In another bowl, stir all the dressing ingredients until thoroughly blended. Or shake in a screwtop jar. Stir into the crab meat mixture.

3 Cut the avocados in half and remove the stones (pits).

4 Place a lightly oiled, ridged, non-stick griddle pan (grill pan) over a high heat and when it's hot, add the avocado halves, cut-side down, pressing down lightly to make contact with the ridges of the pan.

5 Cook for 3–4 minutes until the avocados start to soften and attractive charred stripes appear.

6 Put the avocado halves on 4 serving plates and top with the crab meat mixture. Sprinkle with chopped coriander and serve immediately.

OR YOU CAN TRY THIS...

– Instead of the Thai dressing, stir 2–3 tablespoons mayonnaise and the grated zest and juice of 1 lime into the crab meat mixture.
– Substitute some diced cucumber for the red pepper, and some diced papaya or melon for the mango.
– The topping also works well using prawns (shrimp) or diced chicken instead of crab.

CRAB-STUFFED AVOCADO

SERVES: 4 | **PREP:** 10 MINUTES | **COOK:** 10 MINUTES

150g/5oz (generous ½ cup) white crab meat
150g/5oz (generous 1 cup) fresh soft goat's cheese
1 tsp chopped tarragon
2 ripe avocados
1 tbsp lemon juice
50g/2oz (¼ cup) brown crab meat
4 baby plum tomatoes, thinly sliced
salt and freshly ground black pepper
salad leaves, to serve

Dressing:
1 tbsp walnut oil
2 tbsp olive oil
1 tbsp lemon juice

Soft goat's cheese lends a mild, fresh taste and creamy texture to crab meat. If available, choose small Hass avocados for their nutty flavour.

1 In a bowl, loosen the white crab meat with a fork, removing any pieces of shell. Add half of the goat's cheese and the tarragon. Mix together, seasoning with salt and pepper to taste.

2 Cut the avocados in half and remove the stones (pits). Brush the cut surface of the avocados with lemon juice to prevent them discolouring. Divide the brown crab meat between the avocado halves, spooning it into the cavities.

3 Divide the white crab meat mixture between the avocados, mounding it over the brown meat and spreading it over the avocado.

4 Arrange the sliced tomatoes over the crab. Crumble the remaining goat's cheese on top and season with pepper.

5 Preheat the grill (broiler) to medium. Place the avocados on a baking sheet or in an ovenproof dish and grill (broil) for 10 minutes, until the cheese browns and the avocado is warm.

6 Whisk together the dressing ingredients in a small bowl.

7 Cut the avocados crosswise into thick slices and arrange on a bed of salad leaves on each plate. Drizzle with the dressing and serve warm.

OR YOU CAN TRY THIS...
– If you're in a hurry, instead of making a dressing, just drizzle some balsamic vinegar over the avocados and salad leaves.
– When fresh tarragon is not available, use chives or flat-leaf parsley instead.

GRIDDLED GOAT'S CHEESE & AVOCADO SALAD

SERVES: 4 | **PREP:** 15 MINUTES | **COOK:** 12–15 MINUTES

1 ripe avocado
1 red or yellow (bell)
   pepper, deseeded and
   thickly sliced
1 courgette (zucchini),
   thinly sliced lengthways
olive oil, for brushing
100g/4oz (4 cups) mixed
   rocket (arugula) and baby
   spinach leaves
4 slices baguette (French
   stick)
4 thick slices goat's cheese
   (cut from a log)
1 tbsp pumpkin seeds
salt and freshly ground
   black pepper

Dressing:
3 tbsp olive oil
1 tbsp cider vinegar
juice of 1 lemon
1 tsp Dijon mustard
drizzle of clear honey

This is a twist on the more traditional salad of frisée (curly endive) and grilled (broiled) goat's cheese. The best cheese to use is a chevre blanc log that you can cut into rounds.

1 Mix all the dressing ingredients together in a small bowl.

2 Heat a non-stick griddle (grill) pan over a medium–high heat.

3 Cut the avocados in half, remove the stones (pits) and cut the flesh into quarters. Lightly brush the pepper, courgette and avocado pieces with oil. Place the red pepper in the hot pan and cook, turning occasionally, for 4–5 minutes until tender and slightly charred. Remove from the pan. Add the courgette strips and cook for 1–2 minutes until striped underneath. Turn over and cook the other side. Remove.

4 Add the avocado quarters and cook the cut sides for 2–3 minutes until warm and striped. Remove from the pan and discard the peel.

5 Gently toss the salad leaves in some of the dressing and divide between 4 plates. Arrange the grilled vegetables on top and drizzle with the remaining dressing.

6 Preheat the grill (broiler). Toast the baguette slices and place a round of goat's cheese on each one. Cook under the hot grill (broiler) for 2–3 minutes until the cheese starts to caramelise on top.

7 Place a cheese toast in the centre of each salad and sprinkle with the pumpkin seeds. Season with salt and pepper and serve immediately.

OR YOU CAN TRY THIS...
– Instead of grilling (broiling) the cheese, spread some soft goat's cheese over the toasts, place on top of the salad and drizzle with a little dressing.
– Drizzle the salad with a good-quality balsamic vinegar for sweetness.

WATERMELON & AVOCADO SALAD

SERVES: 4 | **PREP:** 15 MINUTES | **COOK:** 1–2 MINUTES

1 ripe avocado
500g/1lb 2oz peeled watermelon, cut into chunks
4 spring onions (scallions), thinly sliced
175g/6oz (1½ cups) feta cheese, cubed
2 tbsp toasted sunflower and pumpkin seeds
4 mini pitta breads

Dressing:
1 tbsp olive oil
1 tbsp white wine vinegar
few sprigs of mint, chopped

A really light and refreshing starter for a warm summer's day. The saltiness of the feta cheese offsets the sweetness of the melon.

1 Cut the avocado in half, remove the stone (pit) and cut the flesh into cubes. In a bowl, mix together the avocado, watermelon, spring onions, feta and seeds.

2 Whisk the dressing ingredients together until well blended.

3 Pour the dressing over the watermelon mixture and toss gently together.

4 Heat the pitta breads for 1–2 minutes on each side on a hot griddle (grill) pan and then cut into strips.

5 Divide the watermelon mixture between 4 serving plates and serve with the griddled pitta.

OR YOU CAN TRY THIS...

– Arrange a few crisp salad leaves or some bitter white or red chicory (Belgian endive) on the plates underneath the watermelon mixture.
– Instead of salty feta, mix in some cubes of crumbly goat's cheese.
– Substitute chunks of Charentais or cantaloupe melon and cucumber for the watermelon.
– When you remove the rind and seeds from the melon, do it over a bowl and catch the juices, then add these to the dressing.

GRIDDLED CHICKEN CAESAR SALAD WITH AVOCADO

SERVES: 4 | **PREP:** 15 MINUTES | **COOK:** 16–20 MINUTES

2 skinless and boneless
    chicken breasts
olive oil, for brushing
1 ripe avocado
1 head cos (romaine)
    lettuce, separated
    into leaves
4 tbsp finely chopped
    parsley
50g/2oz salad croûtons

Dressing:
4 tbsp olive oil
1 tbsp red wine vinegar
grated zest and juice of
    1 lemon
2 garlic cloves, crushed
few drops of Worcestershire
    sauce
1 raw small egg yolk
25g/1oz (¼ cup) grated
    Parmesan cheese
freshly ground black pepper

Creamy avocado is a great addition to a Caesar salad and perfectly complements the griddled chicken. If you are unwell, pregnant or elderly, leave out the raw egg yolk when making the dressing.

1 Place a ridged non-stick griddle (grill) pan over a medium heat. Brush the chicken breasts lightly with oil and add to the hot pan. Cook for 8–10 minutes each side until golden brown, cooked right through and lightly striped.

2 Remove from the pan and cut the hot chicken breasts into slices.

3 Mix together all the dressing ingredients in a bowl.

4 Cut the avocado in half, remove the stone (pit) and cut the flesh into cubes. Tear the lettuce into bite-sized pieces and mix with the avocado, parsley and croûtons in a large bowl. Pour over the dressing and toss gently.

5 Divide the salad between 4 serving plates and top with the griddled chicken. Serve immediately.

OR YOU CAN TRY THIS...
– Use griddled large prawns (jumbo shrimp) instead of chicken.
– As an alternative to adding the avocado to the salad, mash it into the dressing.
– Sprinkle some more grated Parmesan over the salad before serving.
– For a classic Caesar salad, omit the chicken and mix in some extra croûtons.

WINTER RADICCHIO SALAD WITH AVOCADO

SERVES: 4 | **PREP:** 15 MINUTES

2 heads radicchio or red
   chicory (Belgian endive)
1 ripe avocado
¼ red onion, finely chopped
1 small bunch of parsley,
   chopped
75g/3oz Roquefort cheese,
   diced
1 ripe pear, cored and thinly
   sliced
50g/2oz (generous ½ cup)
   walnuts, roughly
   chopped
salt and freshly ground
   black pepper

Dressing:
4 tbsp olive oil
1 tbsp cider vinegar
juice of 1 lemon
1 heaped tsp honey mustard

This crunchy salad serves four as a starter or two as a main course to accompany a simple plate of cold sliced turkey, chicken or ham and a baked potato. It's great for an impromptu Christmas meal.

1 Slice the radicchio or chicory into thin rounds. Cut the avocado in half, remove the stone (pit), peel and cut the flesh into dice. Mix in a bowl with the onion, parsley and Roquefort.

2 Whisk all the dressing ingredients together and pour most of it over the salad. Toss gently together until well coated.

3 Divide between 4 serving plates and top with the sliced pear and walnuts. Season with salt and pepper and serve.

OR YOU CAN TRY THIS...

– Instead of a pear, use a sweet red-skinned apple. Peel, core and cut into small chunks. Add to the salad before tossing in the dressing.
– Any creamy or crumbly blue cheese works well, including Stilton, Gorgonzola, Dolcelatte and Cambozola, although they lack the intense saltiness of Roquefort.
– At Christmas, add peeled and stoned (pitted) lychees or ruby-red pomegranate seeds.
– Add the juice of an orange rather than a lemon to the dressing.
– This salad is very versatile and you can stir in some sliced spring onions (scallions), snipped chives or chopped pecans. You can even mash the blue cheese with a little crème fraîche and stir into the dressing instead of using cubes.

SCALLOP, BACON & AVOCADO SALAD

SERVES: 4 | **PREP:** 15 MINUTES | **COOK:** 5 MINUTES

4 rashers (slices) extra-thin
    lean back bacon
8 large king scallops
1 ripe avocado
100g/4oz (4 cups) wild
    rocket (arugula)
2 spring onions (scallions),
    chopped
8 cherry tomatoes,
    quartered
2 tbsp vinaigrette dressing
grated zest and juice of
    1 lemon
salt and freshly ground
    black pepper
snipped chives, to garnish

Low in fat and surprisingly 'meaty', scallops are extremely healthy, but you must take care not to overcook them or they will lose their juicy tenderness and become rubbery. For the best results, always use fresh ones if you can get them, but frozen ones will work, too, as long as they're not the queen scallops, which are too small for this starter.

1 With the blade of a knife, stretch out each bacon rasher thinly and then cut them in half. Wrap the scallops in the bacon.

2 Preheat the grill (broiler), line the pan with foil and cook the scallops for about 5 minutes, turning them occasionally, until they are just cooked but still tender and the bacon is crisp and golden brown.

3 Meanwhile, cut the avocado in half, remove the stone (pit), peel and cut the flesh into thin slices, then mix them together the wild rocket, spring onions and cherry tomatoes.

4 Whisk the vinaigrette with the lemon zest and juice and sprinkle over the salad. Toss gently together.

5 Arrange the salad in a little heap on each serving plate and place the bacon-wrapped scallops on top. Lightly season to taste with salt and pepper and sprinkle with chives.

OR YOU CAN TRY THIS...

– You can use frisée (curly endive), baby spinach leaves or any mixture of small salad leaves.
– Quickly pan-fry the scallops with some torn thinly sliced Parma ham or pancetta instead of wrapping them in bacon.
– Omit the bacon and add some pan-fried diced chorizo to the salad.

GREEN QUINOA & AVOCADO SALAD

SERVES: 4 | **PREP:** 15 MINUTES | **COOK:** 15 MINUTES, PLUS STANDING

100g/4oz (scant ¾ cup)
quinoa
270ml/9fl oz (generous
1 cup) vegetable stock
(broth)
75g/3oz curly leaf kale,
chopped
50g/2oz (2 cups) baby
spinach
50g/2oz (2 cups) rocket
(arugula)
1 small bunch of spring onions
(scallions), finely chopped
1 bunch of chives, snipped
few sprigs of coriander
(cilantro), chopped
1 ripe avocado, peeled, stoned
(pitted) and thinly sliced
2 tbsp toasted mixed
seeds, e.g. sunflower and
pumpkin
½ pomegranate, seeds
removed
salt and freshly ground
black pepper

Dressing:
4 tbsp olive oil
1 tsp white wine vinegar
2 tbsp pomegranate molasses
1 garlic clove, crushed
juice of 1 lemon
pinch of allspice

**This is such a healthy way to start a meal – it's packed with vitamins
and minerals, and quinoa is really rich in protein. The addition of
pomegranate molasses and allspice to the dressing gives this salad a
Middle Eastern flavour.**

1 Rinse and drain the quinoa. Bring the stock to the boil in a pan, then
add the quinoa and reduce the heat to a simmer. Cover the pan and
cook gently for about 15 minutes until nearly all the stock has been
absorbed. The quinoa is cooked when the 'tail' pops out of the seed.

2 Turn off the heat and leave the quinoa to steam in the pan, with the
lid on, for 6–8 minutes. Drain off any excess liquid and fluff it up
with a fork. Allow to cool a little.

3 Mix all the dressing ingredients together in a bowl until thoroughly
blended.

4 Stir the chopped greens and salad leaves into the quinoa together
with the spring onions and herbs. Cut the avocado in half, remove
the stone (pit), peel and cut the flesh into thin slices, Gently add the
avocado, taking care not to break the slices, and toss in the dressing.
Season with salt and pepper to taste.

5 Divide between 4 serving plates and sprinkle over the seeds and
pomegranate seeds. Serve warm or cold.

OR YOU CAN TRY THIS...

– You can add virtually any green leaves to this salad – watercress,
young spring greens, etc. – or blanched broccoli florets or diced
cucumber or courgette (zucchini).
– For more crunch, stir in some roughly chopped nuts, such as
hazelnuts or pistachios.
– Make it subtly spicy by adding a good pinch of ground cinnamon
and ginger or some lemony sumac.

TOMATO & PEACH SALAD WITH AVOCADO SALSA

SERVES: 4 | **PREP:** 15 MINUTES | **COOK:** 5 MINUTES

2 large ripe beef tomatoes, thinly sliced

2 large firm ripe peaches, halved, stoned (pitted) and sliced

1 small bunch of chives, snipped, coriander (cilantro) sprigs, and lime wedges, to garnish

Avocado salsa:

1 small ripe avocado

2 spring onions (scallions), chopped

1 small red chilli, deseeded and diced

1 garlic clove, crushed

juice of ½ lime

2 tbsp chopped coriander (cilantro)

1 tbsp extra-virgin olive oil

salt and freshly ground black pepper

Dressing:

1 tbsp caster (superfine) sugar

3 tbsp water

1 tsp lemon juice

½ tsp Dijon mustard

2 tbsp extra-virgin olive oil

salt and freshly ground black pepper

A great starter salad in summer when tomatoes and peaches are in season and at their best. Add a few chive flowers or edible leaves if you have any growing close at hand.

1 Make the avocado salsa. Cut the avocado in half, remove the stone (pit), peel and cut the flesh into dice. Mix all the ingredients together in a bowl. Season with salt and pepper to taste and set aside.

2 Make the dressing: dissolve the sugar in the water in a small pan over a low heat. Bring to the boil and simmer for 3 minutes. Remove from the heat, allow to cool, then stir in the lemon juice and mustard. Gradually whisk in the oil until amalgamated and add seasoning to taste.

3 Arrange the tomato and peach slices in overlapping concentric circles on a large serving plate.

4 Spoon the avocado salsa into the centre and drizzle over the dressing. Sprinkle with chives and garnish with coriander sprigs and lime wedges.

OR YOU CAN TRY THIS...

– Omit the salsa and fan out a thinly sliced large avocado in between the tomato and peach slices.

– Use sliced nectarines instead of peaches.

– Substitute chives, oregano or basil for the coriander.

COUSCOUS SALAD WITH ROASTED BEETROOT (BEETS) & AVOCADO

SERVES: 4 | **PREP:** 15 MINUTES | **COOK:** 30–40 MINUTES

150g/5oz (1½ cups) couscous
240ml/8fl oz (1 cup) boiling vegetable stock (broth)
1 ripe avocado
4 spring onions (scallions), diced
½ cucumber, deseeded and cubed
100g/4oz baby plum tomatoes, quartered
few sprigs of mint, chopped
1 small bunch of parsley, chopped
2 tbsp olive oil
juice of 1 lemon
salt and freshly ground black pepper

Roasted vegetables:
450g/1lb small fresh beetroot (beets), peeled and cut into small cubes
1 red onion, cut into small wedges
olive oil, for drizzling
1 tbsp balsamic vinegar
salt and freshly ground black pepper

Roasted beetroot (beets) and red onions add a hint of sweetness to this salad. Instead of using red beetroot, you could try roasting one of the yellow varieties. This salad is quite filling, so it can be served as a main course with a little chicken, cold deli meats, grilled tuna, tofu or sliced halloumi.

1 Preheat the oven to 220°C, 450°F, gas mark 8.

2 Put the beetroot into a roasting pan with the red onion wedges. Sprinkle over the olive oil and drizzle with balsamic vinegar. Season with salt and pepper and roast in the oven for 30–40 minutes, until the beetroot is tender. Remove and cool.

3 Put the couscous in a large bowl and pour over the boiling stock. Stir well, cover with some cling film (plastic wrap) and leave for 5–10 minutes until the liquid has been absorbed. Fluff up with a fork and leave to cool.

4 Cut the avocado in half, remove the stone (pit), peel and cut the flesh into cubes. Stir the avocado, spring onions, cucumber, tomatoes and herbs into the couscous. Mix with the olive oil and lemon juice and season to taste.

5 Divide between 4 serving plates and top with the roasted vegetables.

OR YOU CAN TRY THIS...

– Use bulgur wheat or quinoa instead of couscous.
– Top with roasted courgettes (zucchini), (bell) peppers, fennel and aubergine (eggplant).
– Add some diced mango and chopped mint for a sweeter, fruity flavour.
– If you're in a hurry, don't bother roasting the vegetables – use some ready-cooked beetroot and flame-roasted peppers from a jar.

CHILLED TOMATO SOUP WITH AVOCADO CREAM

SERVES: 6 | **PREP:** 20 MINUTES, PLUS CHILLING

1.3kg/3lb ripe tomatoes
750ml/1¼ pints (3 cups)
   tomato juice
pinch of sugar
dash of Tabasco sauce
1 tbsp lemon juice
2 tbsp chopped fresh mint,
   plus sprigs to garnish
salt and freshly ground
   black pepper

Avocado cream:
1 large ripe avocado
1 tbsp lemon juice
½ small onion, finely grated
2 tbsp chopped fresh mint
6 tbsp sour cream

This sophisticated soup needs no cooking and is best made with flavourful Italian plum tomatoes, which provide lots of colour, too. Beef tomatoes would be a good substitute if they are very ripe. This soup freezes well but the avocado cream must be made just before serving.

1 Halve the tomatoes, then squeeze out the seeds into a bowl. Reserve 4 tomato halves and cut into fine dice, cover and refrigerate. Strain the seeds through a sieve to extract any juices; discard the seeds.

2 Place the remaining tomatoes in a blender or food processor with all the tomato juice, the sugar, Tabasco, lemon juice and chopped mint. Blitz until smooth, then pass through a sieve into a clean bowl. Season to taste with salt and pepper.

3 Cover and leave for at least 2 hours in the refrigerator to allow the flavours to develop and the soup to become thoroughly chilled.

4 Just before serving, cut the avocado in half, remove the stone (pit), scoop out the flesh and mash it in a bowl with some lemon juice. Stir in the grated onion, mint and sour cream.

5 Stir the reserved diced tomatoes into the chilled soup and ladle into individual serving bowls. Add a dollop of the avocado cream to each one. Garnish with mint sprigs and serve immediately.

OR YOU CAN TRY THIS...
– Substitute fresh basil for the mint.
– Dice the avocado and stir into the soup, leaving out the grated onion. Serve topped with a swirl of sour cream.
– If you're watching your weight, use 0% fat Greek yoghurt instead of sour cream.

CHILLED AVOCADO SOUP

SERVES: 6 | **PREP:** 20 MINUTES, PLUS CHILLING | **COOK:** 15 MINUTES

1 tbsp olive oil
1 onion, finely chopped
3 ripe avocados
600ml/1 pint (2½ cups)
    vegetable stock (broth)
handful of coriander
    (cilantro) leaves and
    stalks, chopped
250g/9oz (1 cup) 0% fat
    Greek yoghurt
juice of 1 lime
salt and freshly ground
    black pepper
olive oil, for drizzling

Tomato salsa:
4 juicy tomatoes, diced
½ red onion, diced
1 red chilli, diced
few sprigs of coriander
    (cilantro), finely chopped
grated zest and juice of
    ½ lime
salt and freshly ground
    black pepper

This velvety chilled soup is perfect for al fresco dining on a warm summer's day. If you're in a hurry, you can chill the soup more quickly by adding some roughly crushed ice cubes.

1 Heat the olive oil in a pan over a low heat. Add the onion and cook, stirring occasionally, for 10–15 minutes until really tender. Take care that it does not brown – it should be golden and translucent. Remove and cool.

2 Cut the avocados in half, remove the stones (pits), scoop out the flesh and put in a blender or food processor with a little of the stock. Blitz briefly and then add the rest of the stock, a little at a time, through the feed tube, blitzing until smooth.

3 Add the cooked onion, coriander, yoghurt and lime juice and blitz again. Season to taste with salt and pepper. Transfer to a bowl, cover and chill in the refrigerator for at least 1 hour.

4 Make the tomato salsa: mix all the ingredients together in a small bowl, seasoning to taste.

5 Serve the chilled soup ladled into bowls, topped with a spoonful of salsa and a drizzle of olive oil.

OR YOU CAN TRY THIS...

– Instead of cooking the onion, blitz some chopped spring onions (scallions) with the avocado and stock.
– Cucumber adds a subtle flavour and makes the soup even more refreshing. Peel, deseed and roughly chop one and blitz it with the avocado.

BLACK BEAN TORTILLA SOUP WITH AVOCADO

SERVES: 4 | **PREP:** 15 MINUTES | **COOK:** 45–50 MINUTES

3 ripe beef tomatoes
2 tbsp olive oil
1 large onion, chopped
2 garlic cloves, crushed
1 hot red chilli, finely diced
good pinch of smoked sweet
    paprika
small bunch of coriander
    (cilantro), chopped
1 x 400g/14oz can black
    beans, rinsed and drained
900ml/1½ pints (3¾ cups)
    vegetable stock (broth)
pinch of brown sugar
salt and freshly ground
    black pepper
4 tbsp sour cream
lime wedges, to serve

Tortilla topping:
1 ripe avocado
75g/3oz tortilla chips,
    roughly crushed
1 hot red chilli, finely diced
50g/2oz (½ cup) grated
    Cheddar or Monterey
    Jack cheese
few sprigs of coriander
    (cilantro), roughly chopped

This spicy colourful soup looks and tastes sensational. It freezes well, so you can make it well in advance if you're entertaining – just prepare the topping and garnishes at the last minute.

1 Preheat the grill (broiler), line the grill pan with foil and place the tomatoes in it. Cook under the hot grill (broiler) for about 15 minutes, turning occasionally, until softened and the skins blacken all over. Once cool enough to handle, remove and discard the skins.

2 Heat the oil in a pan over a low–medium heat. Add the onion and garlic and cook gently for 10 minutes, stirring occasionally, until tender and golden.

3 Add the chilli, smoked paprika, whole tomatoes, coriander and black beans. Cook for 1 minute and add the stock. Bring to the boil, then reduce the heat and simmer gently for 15–20 minutes. Season to taste with brown sugar and salt and pepper.

4 Pour the soup into a blender or food processor and blitz until thick and smooth. Return to the pan and heat through gently.

5 Ladle the hot soup into 4 shallow bowls and swirl in the sour cream. Cut the avocado in half, remove the stone (pit), peel and cut the flesh into slices. Top with the tortilla chips, avocado, chilli, grated cheese and coriander. Serve with lime wedges.

OR YOU CAN TRY THIS...

– As an alternative topping, add a spoonful of guacamole (see page 24) with the crushed tortilla chips.
– If you're in a hurry, add a 400g/14oz can of chopped tomatoes instead of grilling (broiling) fresh ones.
– Reserve some of the black beans to add to the garnish.
– Make the soup into a more substantial 'meal in a bowl' by adding some cooked shredded chicken at the end.

MAIN MEALS

LINGUINE WITH AVOCADO PESTO

SERVES: 4 | **PREP:** 10 MINUTES | **COOK:** 8–10 MINUTES

450g/1lb linguine
1 tbsp olive oil
1 small red chilli,
    deseeded and diced
salt and freshly ground
    black pepper
Parmesan shavings and
    pine nuts, to serve

Avocado pesto:
2 ripe avocados
grated zest and juice of
    1 lemon
2 garlic cloves, crushed
1 small bunch of basil, torn
5 tbsp olive oil
30g/1oz (¼ cup) grated
    Parmesan cheese

Here's a delicious twist on the classic pesto and pasta. Adding avocado makes the sauce more creamy and unctuous. If you don't have a food processor, use a blender, or even a pestle and mortar.

1 Cook the linguine in a large pan of boiling salted water according to the instructions on the packet. Do not overcook – it should be just tender and retain a little 'bite' (al dente).

2 While the pasta is cooking, make the avocado pesto. Cut the avocados in half, remove the stones (pits), scoop out the flesh and put in a food processor with the lemon zest and juice, garlic, basil and olive oil. Pulse until thick and creamy, then stir in the Parmesan.

3 Drain the linguine and return to the hot pan. Add the olive oil and chilli and toss gently. Add the avocado pesto and toss again.

4 Divide the pasta between 4 shallow serving bowls. Grind some black pepper over the top and sprinkle with Parmesan shavings and pine nuts. Serve immediately.

OR YOU CAN TRY THIS...
– This pesto goes really well with spaghetti, tagliatelle or fettuccine.
– You can leave out the chilli, if wished, for a milder flavour, or add the pine nuts to the pesto.
– Try mixing in some cooked large prawns (jumbo shrimp), chunks of salmon or diced ham or chicken just before serving.
– Experiment with different herbs, including coriander (cilantro), rocket (arugula) and chives.

RICE NOODLE, PRAWN (SHRIMP) & AVOCADO SALAD

SERVES: 4 | **PREP:** 20 MINUTES | **COOK:** 5 MINUTES

225g/8oz vermicelli rice
    noodles
1 tsp coconut oil
2 garlic cloves, crushed
juice of 1 lime
450g/1lb (3 cups) peeled
    raw tiger prawns (jumbo
    shrimp)
1 ripe avocado
1 large carrot, cut into thin
    matchsticks
1 cucumber, deseeded and
    cut into thin matchsticks
chopped coriander (cilantro)
    or basil, to garnish

Coconut dressing:
100ml/4fl oz (scant ½ cup)
    coconut milk
juice of 1 lime
1 tbsp Thai fish sauce
1 tbsp palm or brown sugar
1 red bird's eye chilli,
    deseeded and diced
handful of coriander
    (cilantro) or basil leaves,
    chopped
few torn basil leaves

This is a great main course salad for summer – it's colourful, filling, healthy and crunchy. It's also very versatile and you can experiment with different dressings or even top it with sliced griddled chicken instead of prawns (shrimp).

1 Soak the rice noodles in boiling water in a shallow bowl until just tender but still a little firm. Drain well.

2 Make the coconut dressing: whisk all the ingredients together in a small bowl.

3 Heat the coconut oil in a non-stick frying pan (skillet) and cook the garlic for 1–2 minutes. Add the lime juice and then the prawns. Cook over a medium heat for 2–3 minutes, turning occasionally, until the prawns turn pink on both sides.

4 Cut the avocado in half, remove the stone (pit), peel and cut into slices. Put the avocado, drained noodles, carrot and cucumber in a large bowl and toss gently in the dressing.

5 Divide the salad between 4 serving plates and pile the prawns on top. Scatter with chopped coriander or basil and serve.

OR YOU CAN TRY THIS...

– Instead of a coconut dressing, toss the salad in a classic Vietnamese *nuoc cham*: blend the juice of 2 limes with 1 diced chilli, 1 crushed garlic clove and 2 tbsp each of Thai fish sauce and palm sugar.
– Add some beansprouts, thinly sliced red or yellow (bell) pepper or sliced spring onions (scallions) to the salad.
– Toast some sesame seeds and sprinkle over the top before serving.
– If you don't have any Thai fish sauce, use light soy sauce instead.

BARBECUED LA SALAD

SERVES: 4 | **PREP:** 15 MINUTES | **COOK:** 15 MINUTES

olive oil, for brushing

225g/8oz thin asparagus spears, trimmed

1 aubergine (eggplant), thinly sliced

1 red and 1 yellow (bell) pepper, deseeded and cut into strips

8 spring onions (scallions), trimmed

1 small radicchio trimmed and cut into wedges

100g/4oz (4 cups) baby spinach leaves

200g/7oz halloumi, sliced

balsamic vinegar or glaze, for drizzling

salt and freshly ground black pepper

Dressing:
5 tbsp fruity olive oil
juice of 1 lemon
2 tsp Dijon mustard
½ tsp caster (superfine) sugar

Guacamole:
see page 24

In California, salad leaves and vegetables are sometimes thrown on a hot grill. This salad is served with a guacamole but you can just mash an avocado and a crushed garlic clove into the dressing if you prefer.

1 Lightly brush the asparagus, aubergine, peppers and spring onions with oil and place over hot coals on a barbecue or on a heated ridged griddle pan (grill pan). Cook in batches, turning frequently, for 2–3 minutes until just tender but still firm and not too charred. Remove and keep warm.

2 Brush the radicchio with oil and place on the grill. Cook for 2 minutes each side and remove. Toss the spinach leaves onto the grill for just long enough to warm and wilt them, being careful not to overcook otherwise they will stick to the grill.

3 Lastly, grill the halloumi cheese until golden brown on both sides.

4 Mix the dressing ingredients together and pour over the barbecued salad vegetables in a large bowl. Toss gently and season to taste.

5 Divide between 4 serving plates and top with the halloumi cheese. Drizzle with balsamic and serve warm with guacamole.

OR YOU CAN TRY THIS...

– Omit the halloumi and grill (broil) some chicken, prawns (shrimp), salmon or steak.
– Pickled jalapeño chillies will make the salad hotter.

SEVEN-LAYER SALAD IN A JAR

SERVES: 4 | **PREP:** 15 MINUTES

100g/4oz fresh egg noodles
4 celery sticks, sliced
12 radishes, thickly sliced
75g/3oz (1 cup) cooked
    edamame beans
2 small red or yellow (bell)
    peppers, deseeded and
    cut into rings
8 spring onions (scallions),
    sliced
12 slices Chinese leaf
    lettuce, finely shredded
1 ripe avocado
juice of ½ lemon
salt and freshly ground
    black pepper

Dressing:
4 tbsp light soy sauce
1 tbsp rice wine vinegar
4 tbsp no-added-sugar
    peanut butter
water, to mix

The key to making layered salads in jars is to layer the firmer, crisper vegetables at the bottom, put the beans, grains or pasta in the middle and the leafy green vegetables, salad leaves and tender avocado on the top. If you're eating the salad straight away out of the jar, add the dressing last of all; otherwise, always put the dressing at the bottom of the jar and then shake just before eating.

1 Cook the egg noodles according to the instructions on the packet. Drain well and refresh under cold running water. Set aside to go cold.

2 Make the dressing: whisk together the soy sauce and rice wine vinegar and then stir in the peanut butter. If it's too thick, add a little water to thin it and whisk again.

3 Take 4 clean Kilner (glass) jars and spoon a little of the dressing into the bottom of each jar. Next add a layer of the cold noodles, dividing them equally between the jars.

4 Continue layering, adding a layer of celery, then the radishes, edamame beans, peppers, spring onions, Chinese leaf lettuce. If wished, sprinkle some layers with a little salt and pepper as you go. Cut the avocado in half, remove the stone (pit), peel and cut into slices and add as the last layer, sprinkled with a little lemon juice.

5 Pour the dressing over the top of each salad and seal with the glass lid. Serve the salad in the jars and eat with long-handled forks or chopsticks.

– Most vegetables can be added to a salad in a jar; try shredded red cabbage, curly kale, fennel, green beans, peas, diced or sliced cucumber, chopped artichoke hearts and sliced tomatoes.
– Canned chickpeas, kidney, black, borlotti, soya (soy), cannellini, flageolet and butter (lima) beans will add protein and fibre.
– Add a protein layer of sliced or diced cheese, leftover cooked chicken or some cooked tuna or salmon.
– Use rice noodles instead of egg noodles, or even add a layer of couscous, rice, quinoa or bulgur wheat. Anything goes!

GOOD COMBOS

Try one of the following:

MEDITERRANEAN SALAD JAR
Layer up red or yellow (bell) peppers, tomatoes (or sun-blush tomatoes), cannellini beans, artichoke hearts, olives, pine nuts, Parmesan shavings, avocado and rocket (arugula). Dress with a mustardy balsamic vinaigrette.

GREEK SALAD JAR
Layer up chickpeas, red onion, cucumber, tomatoes, feta cheese, black olives, avocado and chopped oregano and mint. Dress with a lemony vinaigrette.

LEBANESE SALAD JAR
Layer up chickpeas, red onion, red (bell) pepper, cooked bulgur wheat, tomatoes, cucumber, avocado and chopped flat-leaf parsley. Dress with a lemony vinaigrette.

SUPERFOOD SALAD JAR
Layer up carrots, sprouting seeds and grains, quinoa, goat's cheese, mixed berries – e.g. blueberries – avocado, flax or pumpkin seeds and baby leaf spinach or kale. Dress with a balsamic vinaigrette.

VIETNAMESE CHICKEN NOODLE SALAD JAR
Layer up carrot matchsticks, chopped spring onion (scallions), cooked chicken, rice noodles, beansprouts, avocado, shredded green cabbage, mint and coriander (cilantro). Make a dressing of Thai fish sauce, rice wine vinegar, fresh lime juice, palm (or brown) sugar, diced chilli and crushed garlic.

GUACAMOLE WHOLE-GRAIN MEAL IN A BOWL

SERVES: 4 | **PREP:** 15 MINUTES | **COOK:** 10 MINUTES

2 tbsp olive oil
1 onion, chopped
2 garlic cloves, crushed
500g/1lb 2oz ready-to-eat mixed grains, e.g. wholewheat, quinoa, lentils, etc.
2 x 400g/14oz cans chickpeas, rinsed and drained
4 tomatoes, chopped
1 tsp harissa paste
salt and freshly ground black pepper
handful of flat-leaf parsley, chopped
griddled flatbreads, to serve

Guacamole:
1 red onion, diced
1 tsp sea salt crystals
2 green chillies, diced
1 garlic clove, sliced
2 ripe avocados
juice of 1 lime
few sprigs of coriander (cilantro), chopped
freshly ground black pepper

Handy pouches of a wide range of ready-to-eat mixed grains and seeds are now available in most supermarkets and delis. They are quick and easy to use as they require no cooking and can be added cold to salads and wraps or heated in soups, casseroles and stir-fries.

1 Make the guacamole: put half of the onion, the salt, chillies and garlic in a pestle and mortar and pound to a rough paste.

2 Cut the avocados in half, remove the stones (pits) and scoop out the flesh. Mash roughly with a fork – keep it chunky, not too smooth – adding the lime juice a little at a time. Stir in the crushed onion mixture, coriander and remaining diced onion. Add a good grinding of black pepper.

3 Heat the oil in a frying pan (skillet) and cook the onion and garlic over a low–medium heat, stirring occasionally, until tender but not browned.

4 Stir in the mixed grains, chickpeas and tomatoes. Cook gently over a low heat for 5 minutes until heated through. Stir in the harissa and season to taste.

5 Divide the mixture between 4 shallow serving bowls and top with the guacamole. Sprinkle with parsley and serve immediately with hot griddled flatbreads, cut into strips.

– You can cook any grains (quinoa, pearl barley, spelt, bulgur wheat, etc.) in the usual way and add them to the onion and garlic.
– If you don't have fresh tomatoes, use canned chopped ones.
– Canned cannellini or butter (lima) beans make a change from chickpeas.
– Instead of making guacamole, top with a diced avocado sprinkled with lemon or lime juice.
– Sprinkle with pomegranate seeds and add a colourful flourish to this dish. Or scatter with some toasted seeds (pumpkin, sunflower, linseeds (flaxseeds)) or pine nuts.
– If you don't have a pestle and mortar to make the guacamole, just mash everything roughly with a fork.
– You can add some diced ripe tomatoes to the guacamole.
– This meal in a bowl tastes great with a spoonful of grainy hummous.
– To make this dish even more substantial, top with sliced griddled chicken or steak, or even a grilled (broiled) salmon fillet.

TIP

The harissa paste is very hot, so add it a little at a time and check the flavour between additions. Alternatively, hand it round separately and let people help themselves.

JERK PRAWNS (SHRIMP) WITH AVOCADO QUINOA

SERVES: 4 | **PREP:** 15 MINUTES, PLUS CHILLING | **COOK:** 20–25 MINUTES, PLUS STANDING

450g/1lb (3 cups) raw shelled tiger prawns (jumbo shrimp)

200g/7oz (generous 1 cup) quinoa

480ml/16fl oz (2 cups) vegetable stock (broth)

1 large ripe avocado

3 tbsp olive oil

6 spring onions (scallions), diced

juice of 1 lemon

handful of parsley, chopped

a few chives, snipped

salt and freshly ground black pepper

For the jerk marinade:

2 tsp allspice berries, crushed

2 tsp black peppercorns, crushed

½ tsp ground nutmeg

½ tsp ground cinnamon

leaves stripped from 4 sprigs of thyme

¼ onion, diced

2 garlic cloves, crushed

2.5cm (1in) piece fresh root ginger, peeled and diced

2 Scotch bonnet chillies, diced

2 tsp brown sugar

1 tbsp soy sauce

juice of 1 lime

This aromatic Caribbean jerk marinade is easy to make in a blender and is well worth the effort. You can also use it to marinate chicken, pork fillet and salmon.

1 Make the jerk marinade: put all the ingredients in a blender and blitz to a paste. Transfer to a bowl and add the prawns, turning them in the paste until well coated. Cover and chill for at least 30 minutes.

2 Rinse the quinoa under cold running water, then drain. Bring the stock to the boil in a pan then add the quinoa. Reduce the heat, cover and simmer gently for about 15 minutes until tender and most of the stock has been absorbed. When the quinoa is cooked, the 'sprouts' or 'tails' will pop out of the seeds. Remove from the heat and leave to steam in the pan, with the lid on, for 6–8 minutes before draining off the excess liquid. Fluff up the quinoa with a fork.

3 Cut the avocado in half, remove the stone (pit), peel and dice the flesh. Mix the avocado with 2 tablespoons of the olive oil, the spring onions, lemon juice and herbs. Season to taste with salt and pepper.

4 Heat the remaining oil in a frying pan or griddle pan and cook the prawns for 1–2 minutes each side until they turn pink. Do not overcook or they will lose their juicy succulence.

5 Toss the quinoa with the avocado mixture, divide the quinoa between 4 serving plates and place the prawns on top. Serve immediately.

OR YOU CAN TRY THIS...

– Vegetarian toppings include grilled (broiled) tofu, roasted beetroot (beets), red onion wedges, (bell) peppers and aubergine (eggplant), or steamed purple-sprouting broccoli and curly kale or spinach.

– Additional flavourings include diced mango or papaya, sun-blush tomatoes, chopped coriander (cilantro), basil and thyme.

VEGETARIAN SLOW-COOKER CHILLI WITH ZINGY AVOCADO SALSA

SERVES: 4 | **PREP:** 20 MINUTES | **COOK:** IN A SLOW COOKER: 4 HOURS HIGH, 8 HOURS LOW

3 tbsp olive oil
1 aubergine (eggplant), cubed
1 onion, diced
3 garlic cloves, chopped
1 large carrot, diced
1 tbsp mild chilli powder
1 tsp ground cumin
1 tsp ground coriander
2 tbsp tomato purée (paste)
2 tsp cocoa powder
1 courgette (zucchini), diced
2 red (bell) peppers,
    deseeded and diced
100g/4oz green beans, cut
    into 2.5cm (1in) lengths
1 x 400g/14oz can chopped
    tomatoes
1 x 400g/14oz can kidney
    beans, rinsed and drained
boiled rice to serve

Zingy avocado salsa:
1 large ripe avocado
10cm (4in) piece cucumber,
    halved, deseeded and diced
few sprigs of coriander
    (cilantro), chopped
4 spring onions (scallions),
    thinly sliced
grated zest and juice of
    1 lime

This is the ultimate vegetarian chilli – so packed with flavour that you'll never miss the meat. If you're a chilli lover, serve a small dish of thinly sliced chillies or some pickled jalapeños alongside for that extra kick.

1 Heat 2 tablespoons of olive oil in a large frying pan (skillet) and cook the aubergine over a high heat for 5 minutes, stirring occasionally, until golden brown. Transfer to the slow cooker.

2 Add the remaining oil to the pan and cook the onion, garlic, carrot and spices over a medium heat for 5 minutes until slightly softened. Stir in the tomato purée and cook for 1 minute before adding the cocoa, courgette, peppers, green beans, tomatoes and kidney beans.

3 Heat through gently and transfer to the slow cooker. Cook for 4 hours on the high setting or 8 hours on low.

4 Meanwhile, make the salsa. Cut the avocado in half, remove the stone (pit), peel and dice the flesh. Mix the avocado with all the other ingredients in a bowl. Season to taste and chill until required, Serve the chilli with some boiled rice with the salsa on the side.

OR YOU CAN TRY THIS...
– Serve with guacamole (see page 24), tomato salsa and sour cream or some grated Cheddar cheese.
– For an alternative to rice, serve with baked potatoes or tortilla chips.
– Use the chilli as a filling for tacos or burritos.
– Cook the chilli on top of the stove in a pan over a low heat until all the vegetables are cooked and tender.

FREEKEH WITH FETA AND AVOCADO

SERVES: 4 | **PREP:** 15 MINUTES | **COOK:** 45–55 MINUTES

300g/10oz (generous 1 cup)
　freekeh
2 tbsp olive oil, plus extra
　for drizzling
1 red onion, diced
1 garlic clove, crushed
2 tsp ras el hanout
2 x 400g/14oz cans
　chickpeas, rinsed
　and drained
225g/8oz baby plum
　tomatoes, halved
1 ripe avocado
175g/6oz (1¼ cups) feta
　cheese, diced
juice of 1 lemon
handful of mint, chopped
4 handfuls of rocket
　(arugula) leaves
2 tbsp toasted pine nuts
salt and freshly ground
　black pepper
Greek yoghurt, to serve

Freekeh, a cereal made from roasted green wheat, is the new super grain. Nutritious, healthy and packed with protein and fibre, it has a deliciously nutty, earthy flavour and coarse texture and can be enjoyed cold as a salad or hot as a pilaff.

1 Soak the freekeh in cold water for 5 minutes and then rinse well. Bring a pan of water to the boil and add the freekeh. Cook for 35–45 minutes until the grains are tender but retain a little 'bite'. Drain well.

2 Heat the oil in a frying pan over a low–medium heat and cook the onion and garlic, stirring occasionally, until softened. Stir in the ras el hanout and cook gently for 1–2 minutes.

3 Add the chickpeas and tomatoes with the drained freekeh and warm through for 3–4 minutes.

4 Cut the avocado in half, remove the stone (pit), peel and dice the flesh. Stir the avocado and feta together with the lemon juice and chopped mint. Season to taste with salt and pepper.

5 Serve on top of the rocket leaves, sprinkle over the pine nuts and add a good spoonful of yoghurt.

OR YOU CAN TRY THIS...
– Add chopped spring onions (scallions), a diced chilli, red, green and yellow (bell) peppers, cucumber, basil, coriander (cilantro) and parsley or chives.
– Serve with harissa or sweet chilli sauce to give this dish a kick.
– Omit the feta and sprinkle with crumbled cheese or Parmesan shavings.
– Add chopped leftover shredded chicken or turkey, roast lamb, diced ham or prawns (shrimp).
– If you don't have any ras el hanout (available from most supermarkets and delis), use a good pinch of ground cinnamon and allspice instead.
– For a stronger flavour, cook the freekeh in some vegetable stock (broth).

TACOS WITH REFRIED BEANS & GUACAMOLE

SERVES: 4 | **PREP:** 15 MINUTES | **COOK:** 15 MINUTES

3 tbsp olive oil

1 onion, diced

2 garlic cloves, crushed

1 red chilli, diced

2 x 400g/14oz cans red kidney beans, rinsed and drained

1 small bunch of spring onions (scallions), diced

8 baby plum tomatoes, diced

handful of coriander (cilantro), chopped

8 taco shells

large handful of shredded iceberg lettuce

1 quantity guacamole (see page 24)

100g/4oz (1 cup) grated Cheddar cheese

salt and freshly ground black pepper

sour cream and lime wedges, to serve

You can buy packs of taco shells in most supermarkets, and they are delicious filled with hot refried beans. If you like, heat them briefly in a medium oven to crisp them up even more.

1 Preheat the oven to 180°C, 350°F, gas mark 4.

2 Heat the olive oil in a frying pan (skillet) and cook the onion, garlic and chilli, stirring occasionally, for about 10 minutes until the onion is tender and golden.

3 Add the beans and heat through. Season to taste with salt and pepper. Tip the mixture into a bowl and mash coarsely with a potato masher.

4 Stir in the spring onions, tomatoes and most of the coriander.

5 Meanwhile, place the taco shells on a baking sheet and heat through in the oven for 3–4 minutes until crisp.

6 Divide the lettuce and refried beans among the taco shells. Top with the guacamole and grated Cheddar, then sprinkle over the remaining coriander. Serve immediately with sour cream and lime wedges.

OR YOU CAN TRY THIS...

– Use black beans or cannellini beans to make the refried bean mixture.

– Stir some diced cooked chicken, turkey or chorizo into the refried bean mixture.

– Fill the tacos with chilli con carne (see page 92) and top with guacamole and sour cream.

– Use shredded cos (romaine) lettuce instead of iceberg.

– Try adding a squeeze of lime juice or some hot salsa.

– Use this filling for warmed tortilla wraps as well as tacos.

– If you're in a hurry, heat some canned refried beans instead and then stir in the spring onions (scallions), tomatoes, coriander (cilantro) and some diced cucumber.

CHEESY AVOCADO FRITTATA

SERVES: 4 | **PREP:** 10 MINUTES | **COOK:** 20–25 MINUTES

2 tbsp olive oil
1 red onion, thinly sliced
2 garlic cloves, crushed
100g/4oz (½ cup) roasted
   peppers (bell or hot
   piquillo), drained and
   cut into strips
large handful of baby
   spinach leaves
8 medium eggs
1 large ripe avocado
50g/2oz (½ cup) grated
   Cheddar or Manchego
   cheese
salt and freshly ground
   black pepper

If you've never thought of adding avocado to omelettes, frittatas and tortillas, try this – its creamy texture and buttery flavour work really well. If you don't want to serve this immediately, allow to cool and then wrap in foil. It makes a good packed lunch and is perfect for picnics.

1 Heat the olive oil in a large non-stick frying pan (skillet) over a medium heat and cook the red onion and garlic, stirring occasionally, for about 6–8 minutes until softened but not browned.

2 Stir in the peppers and spinach and cook gently for 2 minutes until the spinach turns bright green and wilts.

3 Beat the eggs in a bowl with some seasoning. Cut the avocado in half, remove the stone (pit), peel and dice the flesh and stir into the eggs with the grated cheese.

4 Pour the beaten egg mixture into the pan, tilting it to cover the base and sides evenly. Lower the heat to a bare simmer and cook very gently for about 8 minutes, until the frittata is golden brown and set underneath.

5 Meanwhile, preheat the grill (broiler). Put the pan under the hot grill (broiler) and cook for 3–4 minutes until it is golden brown and set on top.

6 Slide the frittata out of the pan onto a plate or board and allow to cool a little. Cut into wedges and serve hot, warm or cold.

OR YOU CAN TRY THIS...

– You can add almost any vegetables to this delicious frittata:
   courgettes (zucchini), mushrooms, cherry tomatoes and diced potato.
– Instead of spinach, toss in a handful of rocket (arugula) or watercress.
– Grated Parmesan gives a more intense flavour than Cheddar.
   Or try some crumbled goat's cheese instead.
– Omit the peppers and stir in some smoked salmon offcuts.

AVOCADO PRAWN (SHRIMP) TEMPURA

SERVES: 4 | **PREP:** 10 MINUTES | **COOK:** 15 MINUTES

sunflower (corn) oil, for
   deep-frying
16 large peeled tiger prawns
   (jumbo shrimp), tail left
   intact
2 medium avocados
boiled rice, to serve
few fresh chives, snipped
soy sauce and wasabi paste,
   to serve

Tempura batter:
150g/5oz (1 cup) plain
   (all-purpose) flour
pinch of bicarbonate of soda
   (baking soda)
250ml/9fl oz (generous
   1 cup) iced water
1 medium egg, beaten

It's not difficult to make your own tempura at home as long as you follow a few simple rules: don't overmix the batter; use iced or very cold water; make the batter at the last minute – not in advance; and check that the oil is at the correct temperature before adding the prawns and avocado.

1 Make the batter: sift the flour and bicarbonate of soda into a large bowl. Lightly whisk in the water and egg until everything is combined. Be careful not to overwhisk the batter – it needs to be lumpy or it will become heavy. Keep the batter cold by placing it over or inside a bowl filled with iced water.

2 Heat the oil in a large saucepan – it should be at least 5cm (2in) deep. When it reaches 190°C/375°F, it's time to start cooking. If you don't have a sugar thermometer to check the temperature, drop a cube of bread into the hot oil. It should be crisp and golden brown within 10 seconds.

3 Holding the prawns by their tails, dip some of them into the batter, shaking off any excess, and then fry in the hot oil for about 3 minutes until crisp and golden. Remove immediately with a slotted spoon to a plate lined with kitchen paper (paper towels).

4 Repeat with the remaining prawns. Cut the avocados in half, remove the stones (pits), peel and cut the flesh into chunks and batter and fry the avocado cubes as you did the prawns.

5 Serve the hot prawns and avocado immediately with some boiled rice, sprinkled with chives and with the soy sauce and wasabi paste alongside.

OR YOU CAN TRY THIS...
– Instead of prawns add vegetables, including red or yellow (bell) peppers, courgette (zucchini), green beans and shiitake mushrooms.
– If wished, add a tablespoon of sesame oil to the tempura batter.
– Serve with a crisp Japanese or Asian-style salad, or some steamed pak choi (bok choy) or greens tossed in soy sauce and grated fresh ginger.

CRAB CAKES WITH AVOCADO TOMATILLO SAUCE

SERVES: 4 | **PREP:** 15 MINUTES, PLUS CHILLING | **COOK:** 20–30 MINUTES

450g/1lb (2 cups) crab meat
2 tbsp mayonnaise
1 red bird's eye chilli, diced
4 spring onions (scallions), diced
3 lime leaves, shredded
1 stalk lemongrass, peeled and diced
small bunch of coriander (cilantro), chopped
50g/2oz (1 cup) fresh white breadcrumbs
1 tsp Thai fish sauce
flour, for dusting
sunflower (corn) oil, for frying
quartered limes, to serve
salt and freshly ground black pepper
Continued opposite

You can use fresh, frozen or canned crab meat to make these spicy little cakes. Serve piping hot with fragrant Thai rice or rice noodles and a crisp salad. Tomatillos can be bought online or from specialist stores, or you can substitute green tomatoes in late summer/early autumn.

1 In a large bowl, mix the crab meat with the mayonnaise, chilli, spring onions, lime leaves, lemongrass, coriander, breadcrumbs and fish sauce. Season lightly with a little salt and pepper. If the mixture is too dry, you can moisten and bind it with some lime or lemon juice or a little beaten egg.

2 Cover and chill in the refrigerator for about 30 minutes.

3 Meanwhile, preheat the oven to 190°C, 375°F, gas mark 5 or the grill (broiler) to high. Put the tomatillos in a roasting pan, drizzle with oil and cook for 15–20 minutes, until softened, in the oven or under the grill (broiler).

4 Cut the avocado in half, remove the stone (pit), peel and cut the flesh into dice. Mix the remaining sauce ingredients together in a bowl and then stir in the roasted tomatillos.

5 With lightly floured hands, divide the crab mixture into 12 portions and shape each one into a little cake.

6 Heat the oil in a pan and cook the crab cakes for 3–4 minutes each side until crisp and golden.

7 Serve immediately with the limes and avocado tomatillo sauce.

Avocado tomatillo sauce:
4 tomatillos, halved
oil, for drizzling
1 ripe avocado
grated zest and juice
    of 1 lime
4 spring onions
    (scallions), diced
good handful of coriander
    (cilantro), chopped

OR YOU CAN TRY THIS...

– If you're in a hurry, serve the crab cakes with sliced avocado
  and some sweet chilli dipping sauce instead of the avocado
  tomatillo sauce.
– To speed up the preparation, just tip all the ingredients for the
  crab cakes into a blender or food processor and pulse briefly.

VARIATION

To make Maryland crab cakes, mix the crab meat with 1 beaten egg,
50g/2oz mayonnaise, 1 tbsp each Worcestershire sauce and Dijon
mustard, a handful of chopped parsley, 50g/2oz (¾ cup) Japanese
Panko breadcrumbs and the juice of 1 large lemon. Season to taste
and chill for 30 minutes before shaping into 4 large or 8 small cakes
and shallow frying as above. Serve with lemon quarters and a sauce
of lemony mayonnaise mixed with mashed avocado, chopped herbs
and 0% fat Greek yoghurt.

CHARGRILLED SQUID WITH AVOCADO & SWEET POTATO

SERVES: 4 | **PREP:** 10 MINUTES | **COOK:** 8–10 MINUTES

olive oil, for cooking

2 large sweet potatoes, peeled and cut into matchsticks

900g/2lb prepared squid, cut into bite-sized pieces

1 large ripe avocado

100g/4oz (4 cups) wild rocket (arugula)

4 tsp toasted pine nuts or pumpkin seeds

sea salt and freshly ground black pepper

Chilli lemon dressing:

2 tbsp fruity olive oil

grated zest and juice of 1 lemon

1 garlic clove, diced

1 fresh red chilli, diced

1 small bunch of chives, snipped

If you're in a hurry or don't fancy preparing the squid yourself, you can buy it ready prepared from most fishmongers and supermarket fresh fish counters. Or use frozen squid (not battered or breaded) and defrost and pat dry with kitchen paper (paper towels) before preparing and cooking.

1 Brush a ridged griddle (grill) pan generously with some olive oil and place over a medium heat. Add the sweet potatoes and cook for about 5 minutes, turning occasionally, until tender and starting to colour and char. Remove and keep warm. Turn up the heat under the pan to high.

2 Toss the squid in a little olive oil and season with plenty of sea salt and freshly ground black pepper. Add to the hot pan and cook for 1–2 minutes each side, until the squid starts to curl up from the heat and is attractively striped.

3 Mix together all the ingredients for the chilli lemon dressing. Toss the hot squid in a little of the dressing and set aside the rest.

4 Cut the avocado in half, remove the stone (pit), peel and thinly slice the flesh. Toss the avocado, rocket and pine nuts or pumpkin seeds in the reserved dressing and divide between 4 serving plates. Top with the sweet potato matchsticks and squid and serve immediately.

OR YOU CAN TRY THIS...

– Cook the sweet potatoes and squid over hot coals on a barbecue for a more smoky flavour.

– Mix some drained canned chickpeas, diced chorizo and griddled baby plum tomatoes or red (bell) peppers into the sweet potato and avocado mixture.

– Prepare the squid in advance and marinate in olive oil, lemon juice, garlic, chilli and seasoning for 1–2 hours before cooking.

– Use lime juice instead of lemon and add 1 teaspoon of Thai fish sauce.

CHILLI CON CARNE WITH AVOCADO SALSA

SERVES: 4 | **PREP:** 15 MINUTES | **COOK:** 30–35 MINUTES

2 tbsp olive oil
1 large red onion, chopped
3 garlic cloves, crushed
2 red (bell) peppers,
    deseeded and chopped
1–2 hot chillies, diced
1 tsp ground cumin
1 tsp chilli powder
500g/1lb 2oz (2¼ cups)
    lean minced (ground)
    beef (max. 5% fat)
1 x 400g/14oz can chopped
    tomatoes
2 tbsp tomato purée (paste)
420ml/14fl oz (1¾ cups)
    beef stock
1 x 400g/14oz can kidney
    beans, rinsed and drained
small bunch of coriander
    (cilantro), chopped
salt and freshly ground
    black pepper
warmed tortillas, salsa and
    sour cream, to serve

Avocado salsa:
1 large ripe avocado
3 ripe tomatoes, diced
1 jalapeño chilli, diced
½ small red onion, diced
juice of 1 lime
handful of coriander
    (cilantro), finely chopped
salt, to taste

Chilli is always a warming and welcoming dish, especially on a cold day. You can make the flavour as mild or as hot as you like, depending on the amount and type of chillies you use. This dish can be prepared in advance and stored in the refrigerator, or even frozen, or you can prepare it the night before and leave it to simmer away gently in a slow cooker.

1 Heat the oil in a large saucepan and cook the red onion, garlic and red pepper over a low heat for 6–8 minutes, stirring occasionally, until starting to soften. Add the chilli(es), cumin and chilli powder and cook for 1 minute.

2 Add the minced beef and cook, stirring, for 2–3 minutes, until broken up and browned. Stir in the canned tomatoes, tomato purée and beef stock and bring to the boil. Reduce the heat, cover the pan and simmer gently for 1 hour.

3 Add the kidney beans and season to taste with salt and pepper. Simmer for a further 20–30 minutes until the sauce has reduced and thickened. Stir in most of the chopped coriander.

4 Just before you are ready to serve the chilli, make the avocado salsa. Cut the avocado in half, remove the stone (pit), peel and dice the flesh, then mix with all the other ingredients in a bowl.

5 Ladle the hot chilli into deep plates or shallow bowls and sprinkle with the remaining coriander. Serve with warmed tortillas, salsa, sour cream and the avocado salsa.

OR YOU CAN TRY THIS...
– Serve with boiled or steamed rice instead of warmed tortillas.
– If you're weight conscious, use virtually fat-free fromage frais or 0% fat Greek yoghurt rather than sour cream.
– Vegetarians can leave out the minced beef and add extra beans, lentils or root vegetables, such as diced sweet potato or swede (rutabaga).

SPICED BEEF WITH AVOCADO TABBOULEH

SERVES: 4 | **PREP:** 20 MINUTES | **MARINATE:** 12 HOURS | **COOK:** 8–14 MINUTES

500g/1lb 2oz fillet of beef,
    all visible fat removed
4 tbsp soy sauce
pinch of ground star anise
2 garlic cloves, crushed
2 tsp diced fresh root ginger
grated zest of 1 lemon
2 tbsp olive oil
salt and freshly ground
    black pepper

Avocado tabbouleh:
150g/5oz (¾ cup)
    bulgur wheat
1 ripe avocado
½ cucumber, diced
4 ripe tomatoes, diced
1 garlic clove, crushed
bunch of spring onions
    (scallions), finely sliced
handful of parsley, chopped
handful of mint, chopped
juice of 1 large lemon
4 tbsp olive oil
salt and freshly ground
    black pepper

A fillet of beef makes a special meal for a family get-together or dinner party. This dish is great in summer, cooked over hot coals on a barbecue. Serve with the tabbouleh and a selection of salads or roasted vegetables.

1 Put the beef fillet in a shallow dish. Mix the soy sauce with the star anise, garlic, ginger and lemon zest, and spoon over the beef. Season with salt and black pepper, then cover the beef and marinate in the refrigerator overnight, or for at least 12 hours.

2 Make the tabbouleh: put the bulgur wheat in a bowl and pour over enough boiling water to cover it. Leave to soak for 15–20 minutes until it swells up and absorbs the liquid. Squeeze out any excess moisture. Cut the avocado in half, remove the stone (pit), peel and dice the flesh. Stir the avocado, cucumber, tomatoes, garlic, spring onions, herbs, lemon juice and olive oil into the tabbouleh. Season to taste.

3 Heat a ridged griddle (grill) pan over a high heat and brush it with the oil. Lift the beef out of the marinade and cook for about 4–7 minutes each side, depending on how rare or well cooked you like it. Ideally, it should be seared on the outside but still slightly pink and juicy inside.

4 Carve the beef into thin slices and serve with the avocado tabbouleh.

OR YOU CAN TRY THIS...

– Substitute quinoa or couscous for the bulgur wheat. Stir in some chopped red onion, quartered baby plum tomatoes, chopped coriander (cilantro) or basil, crumbled feta cheese and diced black olives.
– For an everyday supper, instead of beef, serve the tabbouleh with some griddled chicken breasts or salmon or tuna steaks.

CRISPY DUCK & AVOCADO PANCAKES

SERVES: 4 | **PREP:** 15 MINUTES | **COOK:** 2 HOURS

1 large duck
(about 1kg/2lb 2oz)
sea salt
1 tsp five-spice powder
1 tsp Szechuan peppercorns,
crushed
1 tsp grated fresh root
ginger
16 ready-made Chinese
pancakes
2 ripe avocados
plum sauce or hoisin sauce,
for spreading
½ cucumber, cut into
matchsticks
bunch of spring onions
(scallions), shredded

Duck with avocado is a great combo, so why not use avocado – mashed, sliced or diced – in Chinese pancakes. You can buy ready-made pancakes in most supermarkets as well as specialist Chinese stores.

1 Preheat the oven to 170°C, 325°F, gas mark 3.

2 Rub the duck all over with plenty of salt. Mix together the five-spice powder, crushed peppercorns and ginger, and rub it over the duck.

3 Put the duck in a roasting pan and cook for about 2 hours, checking it regularly and spooning off any fat that runs out of the duck into the pan. This will help to make it really crispy.

4 Turn up the heat to 200°C, 400°F, gas mark 6 for the last 10–15 minutes to make the skin really crisp. Allow the duck to cool a little and then shred the meat with 2 forks. Pile onto a serving plate.

5 Meanwhile, heat the Chinese pancakes in the microwave or the top of a steamer.

6 Cut the avocados in half, remove the stones (pits), peel and roughly mash the flesh.

7 When ready to serve, let everyone help themselves. Spread each pancake with a little plum or hoisin sauce. Add a spoonful of mashed avocado and some shredded duck and top with the cucumber and spring onions. Roll up and eat immediately.

OR YOU CAN TRY THIS...

– Instead of mashing the avocados, dice or thinly slice them.
– To help make the duck skin extra crisp you can pour boiling water over the duck before cooking it. Throw away the water and use kitchen paper (paper towels) to pat the duck really dry before adding the salt and seasoning.

CAJUN CHICKEN BURGERS

SERVES: 4 | **PREP:** 15 MINUTES | **COOK:** 16 MINUTES

4 skinless and boneless
    chicken breasts
1 tbsp olive oil
8 thin rashers (slices)
    streaky bacon or pancetta
4 burger buns, cut in half
2 ripe avocados
few crisp lettuce leaves,
    e.g. little gem or cos
    (romaine)
2 ripe tomatoes, sliced
sea salt and freshly ground
    black pepper

Cajun spice mix:
1 tsp cayenne pepper
1 tsp ground cumin
2 tsp paprika
1 tsp garlic powder
½ tsp dried chilli flakes
½ tsp dried oregano
½ tsp dried thyme
sea salt and freshly ground
    black pepper

The Cajun spice mix can be made in advance and stored in an airtight jar until needed. Make double or treble the quantity and use it for seasoning pork chops, steak or salmon fillets.

1 Mix all the Cajun spice mix ingredients together. Add a little ground sea salt and black pepper.

2 Brush the chicken breasts with the oil and sprinkle with the Cajun spice mix, coating them evenly on both sides.

3 Cook the chicken on a lightly oiled non-stick griddle (grill) pan over a medium–high heat for about 7–8 minutes each side. They should be cooked right through and golden brown and attractively striped on the outside.

4 Meanwhile, grill (broil) or dry-fry the bacon until golden and crisp. Drain on kitchen paper (paper towels).

5 Toast the burger buns lightly. Meanwhile, cut the avocados in half, remove the stones (pits), peel and roughly mash the flesh. Spread the bottom half of each toasted bun with mashed avocado, then add some lettuce leaves and tomato slices.

6 Cut the chicken breasts into thick diagonal slices and arrange on top of the lettuce and tomatoes. Place the bacon rashers on top and cover with the top halves of the burger buns. Serve immediately.

OR YOU CAN TRY THIS...
– Add some ketchup, sweet chilli sauce or some West Indian hot pepper sauce to the burgers.
– Griddle some beef burgers or salmon or tuna steaks instead of chicken, or make some burgers out of leftover cooked chicken or turkey.
– Vegetarians can substitute halloumi or tofu for the chicken.
– Top the burgers with a slice of Emmenthal or Cheddar and flash under a hot grill until the cheese melts.

CHICKEN & AVOCADO TOASTED TORTILLAS

SERVES: 4 | **PREP:** 15 MINUTES | **COOK:** 8 MINUTES

1 large ripe avocado
4 cooked chicken breasts, shredded
bunch of spring onions (scallions), thinly sliced
2 tomatoes, deseeded and roughly chopped
1 red chilli, deseeded and diced
175g/6oz (1½ cups) grated Cheddar cheese
4 tbsp chopped coriander (cilantro)
juice of 1 lime
4 large flour tortillas
olive oil, for brushing
salt and freshly ground black pepper
sour cream and crisp salad, to serve

You can serve these filled tortillas as a main course or a light lunch. They're great party food cut into thin slices and passed round with drinks.

1 Cut the avocado in half, remove the stone (pit), peel and thinly slice the flesh. Mix together the avocado, chicken, spring onions, tomatoes, chilli, cheese, coriander and lime juice in a bowl. Season to taste with salt and pepper.

2 Lay 2 tortillas flat on a chopping board and brush them lightly with oil, then flip over so the oiled side is underneath. Spread the chicken and avocado mixture all over them but not quite up to the edges. Top with the remaining tortillas and press down slightly. Brush the top lightly with oil.

3 Heat a non-stick ridged griddle (grill) pan over a high heat until really hot. Carefully place one of the tortillas on the griddle, oil-side down. Cook for 1–2 minutes until toasted and golden brown underneath, pressing down gently with the back of a large fish slice to help the cheese stick everything together.

4 Use the fish slice to lift the tortilla off the griddle and turn it over. Do this quickly – if you hesitate, it will collapse. Cook on the other side for 2 minutes until golden. Remove from the pan and keep warm while you cook the other tortilla in exactly the same way.

5 Slice the tortillas into wedges and serve with sour cream and a crisp salad.

OR YOU CAN TRY THIS...
– Vary the filling by using diced mozzarella, chopped red onion, diced red, green or yellow (bell) peppers, spinach, mushrooms, refried beans, chickpeas or black beans.
– Instead of chicken, try diced chorizo, shredded turkey or tofu.
– Add some salsa or guacamole to the filling – or even some hummous.

WARM LENTIL AND BURRATA SALAD

SERVES: 4 | **PREP:** 10 MINUTES | **COOK:** 30–35 MINUTES

200g/7oz (1 cup) Puy
or green lentils
2 tbsp olive oil
1 red onion, diced
1 large carrot, finely diced
2 celery sticks, diced
2 garlic cloves, crushed
225g/8oz baby plum
tomatoes, halved
juice of 1 large lemon
1 small bunch of flat-leaf
parsley, chopped
200g/7oz fine green beans,
trimmed and halved
1 large ripe avocado
1 ball of burrata or
mozzarella, torn into
pieces
4 tsp green pesto
salt and freshly ground
black pepper

Lemony dressing:
3 tbsp fruity olive oil
1 tbsp red wine vinegar
juice of 1 lemon
salt and freshly ground
black pepper

Puy lentils are best for this dish, as they keep their shape better than other varieties and do not fall apart or go mushy during cooking. If you can't get Puy, green lentils will do. Red lentils are not suitable here as they cook down to a thick purée. Burrata is a soft cheese, like a creamy mozzarella; use ordinary mozzarella if you can't get it.

1 Put the lentils in a saucepan and cover with cold water. Bring to the boil, cover the pan, reduce the heat and simmer gently for about 20 minutes, until they are just tender but not mushy. Drain well.

2 Meanwhile, heat the oil in a large frying pan (skillet) over a low heat. Cook the onion, carrot, celery and garlic for 8–10 minutes, stirring occasionally, until softened but not browned.

3 Stir in the tomatoes and lentils and cook for 5 minutes, stirring occasionally. If the lentils start to stick, add a little water. Stir in the lemon juice and parsley and season to taste. Remove from the heat and leave to cool a little.

4 Cook the beans in a pan of boiling water for 2–3 minutes until just tender but still crisp. Drain and refresh under cold running water.

5 Make the dressing by mixing all the ingredients together until well blended. Stir into the warm lentil mixture.

6 Cut the avocado in half, remove the stone (pit), peel and thinly slice the flesh. Divide the lentil salad among 4 serving plates and top with the green beans, avocado slices and burrata or mozzarella pieces. Drizzle with pesto and serve warm.

OR YOU CAN TRY THIS...
– Drizzle with a good-quality balsamic vinegar or glaze.
– Try mixing in some diced roasted squash or pumpkin instead of green beans and tomatoes. Serve sprinkled with toasted cumin, pumpkin or sunflower seeds or chopped walnuts or pecans.

SIZZLING STEAK FAJITAS

SERVES: 4 | **PREP:** 10 MINUTES | **COOK:** 12–18 MINUTES

olive oil, for brushing

2 large red onions, thinly sliced

2 red or green (bell) peppers, deseeded and thinly sliced

4 lean sirloin or fillet steaks, all visible fat removed

8 flour tortillas

1 ripe avocado

few crisp cos (romaine) lettuce leaves, shredded

few sprigs of coriander (cilantro), roughly chopped

4 tbsp grated Cheddar cheese

sour cream and guacamole (see page 24), to serve

Hot salsa:

3 large ripe tomatoes, diced

1 hot red chilli, diced

½ red onion, diced

small bunch of coriander (cilantro), finely chopped

juice of 1 lime

sea salt

You can put the sliced or diced avocado on the tortillas before rolling them up or just add a large spoonful of guacamole to the griddled vegetables and steak. Either way, they taste delicious.

1 Lightly brush a non-stick ridged griddle (grill) pan with oil and place over a medium heat. Add the red onions and peppers and cook for 8–10 minutes, turning occasionally, until softened, slightly charred and the onions are starting to caramelise.

2 Remove from the pan and keep warm. Turn up the heat and add the steaks. Cook for 2–4 minutes on each side, depending on how rare or well cooked you like them. Remove from the pan and cut into thin slices.

3 Put the tortillas in the hot pan – just long enough to warm them through. Or you can warm them in the microwave or wrapped in foil in a low oven.

4 Meanwhile, mix all the salsa ingredients together in a bowl.

5 Cut the avocado in half, remove the stone (pit), peel and slice the flesh. Divide the avocado, lettuce, coriander, steak, peppers and red onions on top of the warm tortillas. Add the salsa and sprinkle with grated cheese. Roll up the tortillas and eat immediately with sour cream and guacamole.

OR YOU CAN TRY THIS...

– Chicken breasts make great fajitas, too. Cook on a hot griddle (grill) pan until cooked right through and charred outside.

– Or try grilled (broiled) shelled large prawns (jumbo shrimp).

– Vegetarians can add griddled courgette (zucchini), carrot or sweet potato matchsticks and spring onions (scallions) or asparagus.

DESSERTS & DRINKS

AVOCADO ETON MESS

SERVES: 4 | **PREP:** 15 MINUTES

2 large ripe avocados
1 tbsp icing (confectioner's)
    sugar
juice of ½ lemon
300ml/½ pint (1¼ cups)
    double (heavy) cream
8 mini meringue shells
400g/14oz (2 cups)
    strawberries, hulled
    and quartered

Avocado and strawberries are a surprisingly good combination and are great in salads, too. We've suggested using ready-made mini meringues for speed and convenience, but homemade ones will taste even better.

1 Halve, stone (pit) and peel one of the avocados. Mash the flesh in a bowl until it's really smooth and sweeten with the icing sugar. Stir in the lemon juice to prevent the avocado discolouring. Alternatively, purée everything in a blender or food processor.

2 Whip the cream in a clean, dry bowl until it stands in soft peaks – do not overwhip it. Swirl the cream gently through the avocado purée.

3 Halve, stone (pit), peel and dice the remaining avocado and add to the creamy mixture.

4 Break the meringue shells into large pieces and stir into the mixture with the strawberries, reserving a few for decoration.

5 Divide the mixture between 4 serving bowls or sundae glasses and serve immediately, decorated with the reserved strawberries.

OR YOU CAN TRY THIS...

– Decorate with sprigs of fresh mint and dust with icing sugar. Or sprinkle with dried rose petals (now available from many supermarkets and delis).
– You can add other berries, including raspberries, blueberries or redcurrants.
– For a lower-fat version, use 0% fat Greek yoghurt instead of whipped cream, or mix it with a little creamy mascarpone.

CHOCOLATE AVOCADO MOUSSE

SERVES: 4–6 | **PREP:** 10 MINUTES | **COOK:** 4–5 MINUTES

2 large ripe avocados
3 tbsp cocoa powder
squeeze of lime juice
few drops of vanilla extract
3 tbsp agave syrup
75g/3oz (⅓ cup) coconut
   cream
100g/4oz plain (semisweet)
   chocolate (70% cocoa
   solids)
plain (semisweet) chocolate
   shavings and fresh fruit,
   such as berries, coconut
   flakes or orange segments,
   to decorate

Don't be put off by the idea of adding avocado to a chocolate mousse. You can't taste the avocado, but it lends this mousse a marvellous velvety texture – and it's dairy-free.

1 Halve, stone (pit) and peel the avocados. Scoop out the flesh and put it in a food processor or blender with the cocoa powder, lime juice, vanilla extract, agave syrup and coconut cream. Blitz briefly until you have a smooth purée.

2 Melt the chocolate in a bowl suspended over a pan of simmering water, making sure the bottom of the bowl isn't touching the water. Once the chocolate is melted, remove the bowl from the heat and allow to cool slightly.

3 Pour the melted chocolate into the avocado mixture and blitz with a hand-held blender until thoroughly mixed, smooth and creamy.

4 Spoon into 4 serving glasses and serve sprinkled with chocolate shavings and decorated with fresh fruit.

OR YOU CAN TRY THIS...
– Use liquid honey or maple syrup instead of agave, or sweeten to taste with artificial sweetener.
– Top with fresh strawberries, raspberries, orange or clementine segments, or some coconut flakes.
– You can also add 4 stoned (pitted) dates to the avocado mixture in step 1.

AVOCADO ICE CREAM

SERVES: 6 | **PREP:** 10 MINUTES, PLUS CHILLING | **COOK:** 10–15 MINUTES

2 egg yolks
150g/5oz (generous 1 cup)
    caster (superfine) sugar
600ml/1 pint (2½ cups)
    full-fat milk
4 ripe avocados
grated zest and juice of
    1 lemon
grated zest and juice of
    1 lime
2–3 drops of vanilla extract
fresh strawberries, to serve

If you have an ice-cream maker this dessert is much easier to make and will be smoother and more velvety than if you did all the mixing by hand.

1 Beat the egg yolks and sugar together in a large bowl until pale and creamy.

2 Heat the milk in a heavy-based saucepan until it nearly reaches boiling point. Pour the hot milk onto the egg and sugar mixture, whisking until well combined, and then tip it back into the pan.

3 Cook very gently over a low heat, stirring with a wooden spoon, until the custard thickens and coats the back of the spoon. Remove from the heat and leave to cool.

4 Halve, stone (pit) and peel the avocados. Scoop out the flesh and put it in a blender or food processor with the lemon and lime zest and juice and vanilla extract. Blitz until you have a smooth purée. Add the cooled custard and blitz briefly.

5 If you have an ice-cream maker, add the avocado mixture and churn until frozen and smooth.

6 Alternatively, pour the avocado mixture into a plastic container or deep baking dish, then cover and freeze for 3–4 hours, stirring it at least once every hour to break up any ice crystals that form.

7 Remove from the freezer and transfer to the refrigerator about 10–15 minutes before serving to soften the ice cream a little. Serve with fresh strawberries.

OR YOU CAN TRY THIS...
– For a richer ice cream, use half milk and half double (heavy) cream to make the egg custard.
– Or you can substitute coconut cream for some of the milk.
– Serve with chocolate shavings or sprigs of mint and sliced mango.

AVOCADO SMOOTHIES

Avocados add a silky, velvety texture as well as vitamin E, potassium and fibre to a range of healthy smoothies. Whip them up for a quick, nutritious breakfast or power snack. They're a great way to get your daily quota of fruit and vegetables as well as helping to lower your cholesterol and give you energy. Green smoothies are particularly healthy because blending the vegetables breaks down their cellulose structure and makes it easier for us to absorb the nutrients.

1 small ripe avocado
handful of kale leaves, trimmed and shredded
handful of baby spinach leaves
handful of fresh mint leaves
1 kiwi fruit, peeled and sliced
2 pears, peeled, cored and cut into pieces
coconut water, to mix

AVOCADO AND KALE SMOOTHIE

SERVES: 1 | **PREP:** 10 MINUTES

This is the ultimate green smoothie. You can vary the flavour by using different fruits, including pomegranate seeds, dessert apples and banana.

1 Cut the avocado in half, remove the stone (pit) and peel. Put the flesh in a blender with the kale, spinach and mint leaves and blitz briefly to a green purée.

2 Add the prepared fruit and blitz again until smooth. Add just enough coconut water to mix to the right consistency and pulse quickly.

3 Pour into a tall glass and drink immediately.

½ ripe avocado
100g/4oz (½ cup)
    strawberries, hulled
150ml/¼ pint (generous
    ½ cup) milk, plus extra
    (optional)
5 tbsp 0% fat Greek yoghurt
drizzle of honey

CREAMY STRAWBERRY & AVOCADO SMOOTHIE

SERVES: 1 | **PREP:** 5 MINUTES

Adding some dairy to a smoothie makes it deliciously creamy. This can be eaten as a breakfast, snack or even a dessert.

1 Cut the avocado in half, remove the stone (pit) and peel. Put the flesh in a blender with all the other ingredients and blitz until smooth. If it's too thick for your liking, add a little more milk to get the desired consistency.

OR YOU CAN TRY THIS...

– Add a mashed small banana to avocado and fruit smoothies. It adds flavour and a thicker consistency.
– Experiment with different fruit – mango, papaya, blueberries, raspberries, peaches, melon and even dried prunes all work well.
– You can thin fruit smoothies with a little orange or apple juice.
– A little lemon or lime juice will help prevent green smoothies discolouring as well as adding a citrusy flavour to the mix.
– Adding some low-GI oatmeal will make the smoothie more filling and help to keep you going for longer, releasing energy slowly and keeping food cravings at bay.
– Add a spoonful of bran for extra fibre or some raw almonds, walnuts, chia or flaxseeds.
– Instead of regular milk, try coconut, almond, soy, oat, hemp or rice milk.
– If you're weight-conscious, use skimmed or semi-skimmed milk.
– When making green vegetable smoothies, add a celery stick, some flat-leaf parsley, pak choi (bok choy), cucumber or some carrot juice.
– To sweeten smoothies, try clear honey, agave or maple syrup, or some liquid artificial sweetener.
– A pinch of ground cinnamon or some grated fresh root ginger will spice up your drinks.
– Flavour your smoothies with a dash of vanilla extract.